a behavioral approach to counseling

marriage happiness

david knox, ph.d.

EAST CAROLINA UNIVERSITY

RESEARCH PRESS COMPANY
2612 NORTH MATTIS AVENUE
CHAMPAIGN, ILLINOIS 61820

Library of Congress Catalog Card Number: 72-075100

ISBN 0-87822-054-2

to frances

**who has made
happiness in marriage
a reality**

"Grow old along with me!
The best is yet to be,
The last of life,
For which the first was made..."

ROBERT BROWNING

acknowledgements

No book, large or small, is the product of one writer. Many persons have assisted in many ways in the development of this behavioral approach to happiness in marriage. Charles Madsen, Jr. has been the most encouraging influence in the creation of this short work. Much of the following has been written in consultation with him and is reflective of his creative thinking. To him, I am most humbly indebted.

Jack Turner, John Greene, Everett Hagerty, James Croake, William Eastman, Arnold Lazarus, Thomas D'Zurilla, Leonard Krasner, Gerald Davison, and Robert Liebert have shared their invaluable clinical skills and experiences in the management of human behavior. Thomas D'Zurilla and Leonard Krasner read the manuscript and made critical suggestions regarding content and structure. To my companions in learning, I am indebted to Steven Fishman, Barry Lubetkin, and James McGee for a personally and professionally rewarding experience in the behavior modification program at Stony Brook.

Behavioral techniques offer marriage counselors an impressive array of useful procedures. These have been developed by countless scientific investigators who studied, experimented, questioned, and carefully redesigned studies prior to their application to marital interaction. Their arduous labors have made possible a behavioral approach to marriage happiness.

Grateful acknowledgement is expressed to Anne Smith for her careful typing of the final manuscript and to Sherrel Hissong for her care and enthusiasm in editing the final manuscript.

To Frances, my wife, my greatest appreciation is expressed for typing the original manuscript and for making our goal of happiness a reality.

David Knox
Stony Brook, New York
Summer, 1971

contents

introduction

With the notable exceptions of Stuart (1969, 1971), Thomas, Carter, and Gambrill (1969), Goldstein and Francis (1969), and Patterson and Weiss (Weiss, 1971), the efficacy of the systematic application of behavioral procedures to marriage problems has not been clarified through research. But their work coupled with case studies (Madsen, 1969; Liberman, 1970; Knox, 1970) and theoretical presentations (Lazarus, 1968; Rappaport and Harrell, 1971) suggests the usefulness of behavioral techniques in resolving problems which plague the husband-wife relationship. Both counselors and spouses may profit from a continued exploration of a behavioral approach to marital happiness.

The text is presented in three parts. Part One, A Behavioral Approach, outlines important perspectives, decisions, and selected specific techniques inherent within the behavioral framework. The reader is encouraged to continually ask practical questions and look forward to Part Two, Problems in Marriage, which classifies problems into general categories found to be common (singly or in combination) in most marriages. Specific examples with alternative treatment procedures are presented for illustrative purposes. Part Three, Application, consists of cases chosen from the writer's files which illustrate the application of behavioral procedures to marriage counseling.

PART ONE

A BEHAVIORAL APPROACH

A major thesis of this book is that marriage counselors should focus primarily on the measurable and potentially measurable behaviors (broadly defined to include overt, cognitive, and physiological responses) of their clients. Since the goal of most couples who seek marriage counseling is "happiness," counselors might best use their therapeutic time by identifying the behaviors which produce happiness, delineating the conditions which influence these behaviors, and systematically structuring the environmental contingencies of which these behaviors are a function. Most couples are very pleased with the focus upon behavior:

> . . .how should one know that he is loved but by the way people act toward him: what they say, how they look, how they touch, in a word, what they DO? Attention, praise, spoken niceties, and physical contact have been demonstrations of love for years. Who cares if someone loves them if they never receive evidence through attention, contact, or the spoken word? (Madsen and Madsen, 1970–1971)

Part One details the assumptions of the behavioral clinician about the etiology of human behavior and his notion of how behavior can be changed to influence human happiness. Included is a discussion of the decisions spouses should make regarding their own values which will determine the goals of therapy.

Marital happiness does not occur by chance. A happy husband and wife are happy because of what their partner says and does. A behavioral approach is concerned with initiating and maintaining the behaviors which result in marriage happiness.

1. perspectives

MARITAL BEHAVIOR IS LEARNED

Cross-cultural research on marriage and family patterns has demonstrated that cultural, social, and psychological learning variables play an important role in determining marital behavior (Mead, 1939, 1949; Stephens, 1957; and Mace, 1960). A bride and groom bring to their marriage cultural heritages and reinforcement histories which will influence how they think, feel, and act toward each other. Not only do spouses learn marital role behaviors from their parents, relatives, peers and mass media, but, more importantly, they are students and teachers of each other as well.

Marital behavior rarely occurs independent of its consequences. Rather, the outcome of a behavior will often increase or decrease the probability that the behavior will recur. A wife who thanks her husband for calling to say that he will be delayed in getting home increases the probability that he will call when he is late again. On the other hand, the wife who scathes her husband, "If you were any kind of a husband or father, you would be here now," is probably not only insuring that he will not call the next time, but also that "next time" will occur sooner and more frequently. Other ways in which spouses influence each other are illustrated in subsequent chapters.

GOALS OF THERAPY

It is helpful to specify marital problems in terms of specific behaviors. A spouse's problems are defined in terms of behaviors that either mate would like terminated, decreased or increased, modified, or perhaps, developed. For example, some husbands may report a desire (goal) to stop premature ejaculation (therapy goal), while other husbands may indicate that nagging behaviors should terminate (decrease negative and increase positive verbal statements). Some wives may want to enjoy sex (achieve orgasmic behavior), while others may report a desire to have their husbands' drinking behaviors controlled (terminate noncontrolled and initiate controlled drinking). Behavioral specification of problems may also involve cognitive behavior. Recently, a husband of four years noted that he no longer loved his wife and wanted to learn to recreate this emotion. The behavioral objective of treatment became the cognition "I love you."

PROCESS OF THERAPY

The pinpointing of specific behaviors is followed by the spouses keeping accurate records of their behaviors. How often and under what conditions do premature ejaculation, no orgasm, "nagging," and drinking alcohol occur? No one knows (not even the client) unless these behaviors are recorded. To assist in the recording procedure, spouses are given blank charts to record the frequency of various behaviors and a sample of their "at home" interaction.[1] These charts are helpful not only in deciding what contingencies to establish but also in evaluating changes over time. (See Charts 1 through 8.)

Following the pinpointing and recording of behaviors, the stimulus variables which influence the behaviors are manipulated. This may involve the counselor establishing external environmental contingencies, by using a variety of techniques, in order to produce the desired behavior in his clients. It may also involve getting the clients to manipulate

---

[1] Counselors may suggest **Keeping Happiness In Marriage: A Positive Approach** (written for couples; available from Research Press Co., 1972) which explains a behavioral perspective of marriage and includes charts, instructions, etc.

behavioral record

WEEK OF _March 21-28_

BEHAVIOR BEING OBSERVED

Ejaculation

OBSERVED BY

_Mr. H._

CHART 1

Mr. H. delayed ejaculation for two minutes of four occasions.

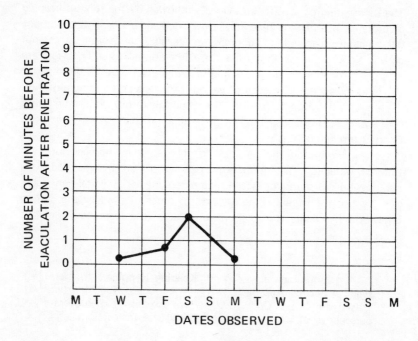

behavioral record

WEEK OF _March 21-28_

BEHAVIOR BEING OBSERVED
Orgasm

OBSERVED BY
Mrs. H.

CHART 2
Mrs. H. recorded one orgasm of four sexual experiences.

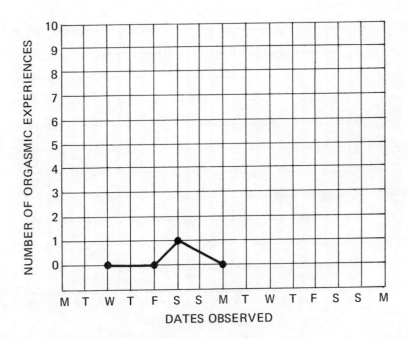

behavioral record

WEEK OF _April 1-7_

BEHAVIOR BEING OBSERVED

Compliments from wife

OBSERVED BY

_Mr. B._

CHART 3

Mrs. B. complimented Mr. B. on 19 occasions in one week.

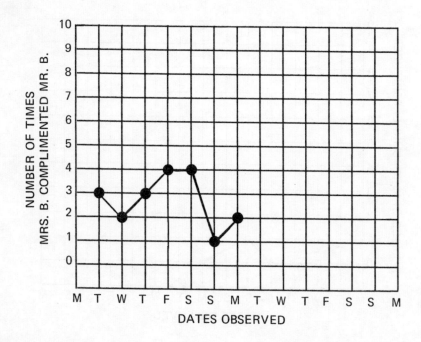

8

behavioral record

WEEK OF *April 1-7*

BEHAVIOR BEING OBSERVED

Controlled drinking of alcohol

OBSERVED BY

Mrs. B.

CHART 4
Mr. B. had 5 days of "controlled drinking."

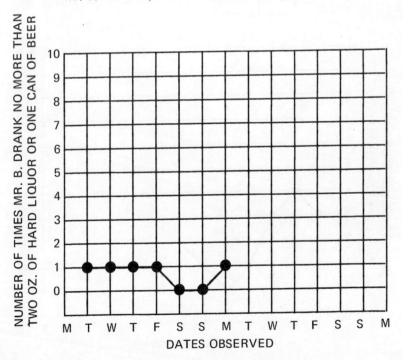

behavioral record

WEEK OF *May 10-17*

BEHAVIOR BEING OBSERVED

Time with my wife

OBSERVED BY

Mr. D.

CHART 5
Mr. D. spent 12 hours during the week and 2 hours during the week-end with his wife.

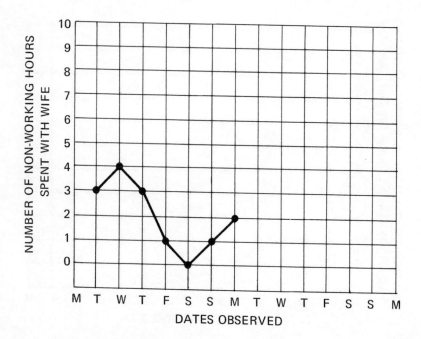

behavioral record

WEEK OF _May 10-17_

BEHAVIOR BEING OBSERVED
"Affection"

OBSERVED BY
Mrs. D.

CHART 6
Husband engaged in "affectionate" behavior once.

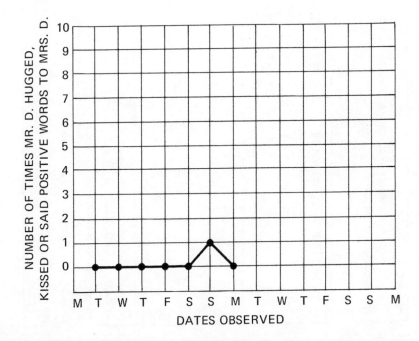

CHART 7

Husband records his response to specific desirable and undesirable behaviors of his wife.

husband's observations

DAY _Saturday_

DATE _March 20_

WIFE'S DESIRABLE BEHAVIOR	WIFE'S UNDESIRABLE BEHAVIOR	YOUR RESPONSE TO HER BEHAVIOR
	Nagged me about cleaning basement, washing her car, repairing the draperies.	"Shut up"
	Refused intercourse	"I can get it elsewhere"
	Emptied my liquor bottles	cut down her nose break
Served delicious supper - steak, potatoes, salad, fresh green peas, wine etc.		Kissed her and suggested that we see a movie
Was ready to leave for movie "on time."		"I can't believe you're ready"

12

CHART 8

Wife records her response to specific desirable and undesirable behaviors of her husband.

wife's observations

DAY _Saturday_

DATE _March 27_

HUSBAND'S DESIRABLE BEHAVIOR	HUSBAND'S UNDESIRABLE BEHAVIOR	YOUR RESPONSE TO HIS BEHAVIOR
	Failed to lock front and back doors before coming to bed last night.	"That's the third night in a row."
Said he enjoyed beef casserole.		"It's about time you liked something."
	Told me he hated my mother.	Cried.
Called me at 5:00 P.M. to tell me he would be late for supper.		"Thanks you for calling. See you at seven."
Told me he thought I was a good wife.		Smiled, kissed him, and led him to the bedroom.

13

certain contingencies so as to influence each other's behavior. The application of these various procedures is illustrated in Parts Two and Three.

Unless records are kept, it is impossible to know if the goals of therapy are being achieved. Clients should continue to keep records throughout therapy to ascertain if the desired changes are occurring. If desirable changes are not developed, new manipulations must be carried out until success is achieved.

When possible, the husband and wife are seen together. The insistence on involving both spouses in therapy has two effects: (1) The "problems" are considered to be "unit" problems which encourage a joint effort to resolve the experienced difficulty; and (2) the notion of a "sick" spouse, presumably responsible for the marital unhappiness, is obviated.

Couples who seek marriage counseling vary in their motivation to maintain their relationship. Some couples sit close together and exchange affectionate, supporting words. These "committed" couples usually identify a specific problem they have had difficulty in resolving. Examples include premature ejaculation, impotence, frigidity, etc. The therapist's role is to provide specific directives to alleviate their distressed impasse. (See Case 5.)

In contrast to committed couples, "deadlocked" couples often consider the marriage counselor their last chance before the lawyer. Many spouses are still pliable and willing to compromise for mutual happiness. (See Case 12.) Others are embittered and have little interest in maintaining their marriage. When a compromise is not possible, the counselor may focus on the partner more committed to the marriage. By increasing the desirable behavior of the more committed spouse, the mate often experiences renewed interest in the marriage and becomes more willing to compromise. (See Case 11.)

THE WHOLE PERSON

Behavior therapy is sometimes presumed to be preoccupied with limited circumscribed behaviors or sequences of behavior with subsequent neglect of the total person as he interprets his environment. Behavior as defined refers to any measurable or potentially measurable human response. As noted previously, this includes not only overt behavior but cognitive and physiological processes as well. The efficacy of treatment is improved by dealing specifically with all three types of personal reactions. A husband who interprets his wife's yelling as an attempt to get his attention will respond differently from the husband who interprets the same yell as intimidation or scorn. In a similar way, if a husband reacts with extreme "anxiety" (physiological arousal) to his wife's anger, his response may be different from that of a less "sensitive" person. Hence, within the behavioral framework, cognitions and physiological reactions are considered as important as overt behavior.

INSIGHT AND BEHAVIORAL CHANGE

Problems arise when it is assumed that insight must always precede behavioral change. The relationship between overt behavioral change and insight (covert behavioral change) is like the proverbial story of the chicken and the egg. In many cases, overt change may precede covert change. A university senior noted that he had not asked a girl for a date for three years because he had assumed that a college degree was necessary before a girl would accept. Finally, in desperation and loneliness, he asked a coed in his tennis class for a date, which she graciously accepted. The "insight" then occurred to him that his assumption had been erroneous.

Other examples, however, indicate that "insight" may, indeed, effectively induce overt behavioral change. Lazarus (1970) noted the treatment of a client who had been involved with a behavior therapist in therapy for impotence. Systematic desensitization and other behavioral techniques had been utilized to no avail. During a discussion of sex, Lazarus discovered the patient's misconception that "vaginas have the capacity to squeeze the penis off." Until the thoughts (covert behaviors) were changed ("insight"), therapeutic successes were limited. Insight as used here refers primarily to a misconception which differs from the traditional psychodynamic view of "insight" as understanding and accepting the presumed etiology and dynamics responsible for one's symptoms. It is important to distinguish between the identification of cognitive distortions (acceptable to behaviorists) and "insight" in the traditional sense (unacceptable).

Counselors should be concerned with both behaviors and cognitions (Greene, 1970; Lazarus, 1971). In some cases, a cognitive restructuring process may be necessary before lasting behavioral changes can be effected. A change of cognitions may both facilitate other behavioral changes (overt) and may, perhaps, be involved in the inducement of more permanent changes (Lazarus, 1971).

THERAPEUTIC RESPONSIBILITY

Disgruntled marital partners who choose to improve their marriage and who know how to do so do not seek marriage counseling. Partners not successful in resolving their problems make an appointment in the hope that positive changes will occur. The therapist then directly intervenes to help the spouses define and reach appropriate goals. This includes specifying the behavioral referents for such presenting problems as "Our sex life is bad," "John is moody," "We're not happy," etc., and choosing from an array of procedures to accomplish the client's goals. Of course, the availability of a technique does not imply that the effective therapist does not involve himself in a very personal way with his clients.

Behavior therapy, particularly as applied to marriage counseling, is a relatively new phenomenon. In regard to the new movement of behavior therapy, Paul (1966) indicated that both desirable and undesirable consequences follow from a flood of innovations. He explained that "new techniques may be prematurely adopted, or rejected out-of-hand when innovations roll in so fast that evaluation of their effectiveness never gets beyond the case study stage."

When behavioral principles are applied to the problems of marriage relationships, the achievement of happier marriages may result. The therapist should never deceive himself into thinking that he can intervene in a marriage without influencing the behavior of the marital partners. He will have a direct influence and, therefore, should plan carefully, deliberately, and take responsibility for his intervention.

2. decisions

Ellis (1962) and Lazarus (1971) have noted the important influence of cognitions on behavior. Since most marital discord involves a junk yard of faulty cognitions and misconceptions, restructuring the psychological world of the couple becomes a major therapeutic goal. This involves making a systematic investigation of the basic assumptions which underlie the respective response patterns of the husband and wife and assisting them in making decisions relative to the modification, development, and acceptance of more adaptive "rules" and cognitions.

PROBLEM DISCRIMINATION

A problem is a situation which demands a solution (Johnson, 1971). Considerable guilt, worry, disappointment, and frustration result from the inability of a client to discriminate "who has the problem" in any given situation. A wife recently said that her parents did not like her husband because he was a "no good mechanic." She was distraught at her parents' rejection of a man whom she both admired and loved. When asked if she felt that her parents were justified in their accusations, she replied tearfully, but firmly, "No." The counselor then assisted her in recognizing

17

who had the problem. Her parents had chosen not to accept her husband, although he was quite acceptable to her. It was unfortunate that their marriage was not approved of by her parents, but parental approval is not essential for a happy life together. The wife, when seen a few days later, said that she had decided not to see her parents again unless they would agree to accept her husband. She had made a value decision in which she had chosen her husband over her parents (a crucial decision) and had clearly discriminated who had the problem.

The need for problem discrimination may be very subtle. A husband, content in his own marriage, may be talking with a disgruntled and miserably unhappy married man who extols the advantages of the divorced. Inadvertently, the "happily" married man may begin to take the problem of the dissatisfied husband and think negatively about his own marriage. Hence, the discrimination of who has the marriage problem becomes crucial.

In happy, productive marriages, each spouse often makes the decision to take the problem of the partner as a problem of his own (Madsen, 1968). A husband will usually assist his wife during pregnancy, just as she will lessen his problem of sickness by caring for him. One of the first goals of counseling is the partner's recognition and acceptance of each other's problems. His drinking becomes a problem which she must cope with as her feelings of loneliness and rejection become a problem for him. The decision to assist the partner with the problem often ameliorates the resentment of the presence of the problem. Partners who choose not to take the problem of the other will profit little from therapy.

However, there are times when taking the problem of the partner is dysfunctional. Husbands often feel they must assist their wives in the preparation of food and the washing of dishes, which may result in role confusion. The role responsibilities of a couple recently in treatment were such that for any given evening meal, it was not clear who was responsible for what. As a result, each would scathe the other with, "I thought you were taking care of that."

To assist in clarifying role behaviors, the wife was made responsible for all matters pertaining to meal preparation. The husband was instructed to stop cooking, washing dishes, and buying groceries. Instead, he became solely responsible for other duties in which she had been involved. The implementation of these new role behaviors became possible through the agreement that should either fail in their respective role responsibilities, each was not to take the problem of the other. If the wife "forgot" to prepare a meal, the husband was not to assist her with the meal or take her out to eat. Meal preparation was now her responsibility— her problem. In the same way, if the car needed to be serviced, it was the husband's problem. Therapy proceeds at a faster rate by the clarification of separate and distinct role behaviors. The decision of when and when not to take the problem of the partner is crucial.

VALUES

Each spouse has learned a unique set of values (behavioral preferences). Observable behaviors reflect the respective value system of each partner. A wife who enrolls in a ceramics class, creates new cake recipes, grows flowers, and reads **Love Story** is said to value ceramics, cooking, flowers, and reading. If she said she did not value these things, the therapist should point out the discrepancy between her behaviors and words. It is easy to ascertain where the husband is arranged in the value hierarchy of the wife by observing what she DOES for and with him. A wife who chooses to spend her time grading papers when her husband would like to talk, take a drive, or have intercourse and who says that she values her husband over her school work is deceiving herself.

In the same way, a husband often deceives himself about the hierarchal value placement of his job and wife. Many husbands love their wives so much that they work at the office every night. Other husbands love their wives so much that they take their vacations without them, and often with a mistress. The therapist should clarify the existing values of the spouses by making reference to specific behaviors. The partners may then decide to change their values (husband will spend more time with his wife) or achieve acceptance from the spouse for their existing values (the wife will stop asking her husband when he will be home).

These alternatives become crucial since the wife, through observation of her husband's behaviors, will know what his values are and whether or not he is making an effort to change. If she values a husband who spends some evenings with her and yet continues to live with a husband who does not, she is deceiving herself and reinforcing his behavior.

Throughout therapy, the counselor should communicate to his clients that their behaviors reflect their values. Clients who do not keep record sheets or perform "homework" assignments are reminded of the negative consequences. Spouses who do not conscientiously work toward resolving their problems keep them.

Of course, clients often do not perform the suggested behaviors of therapy because the directions are not clear or they are "afraid." To obviate confused directions, the counselor writes down his suggestions, discusses them in detail, and gives the clients a copy. Fear of performing "homework" assignments can be minimized by suggesting graduated behavioral changes which may be role played and rehearsed again and again until the client is "ready."

LIFE AS THE STOCK MARKET

Investors and non-investors know that Wall Street is a market place of winners and losers. While some investors peruse prospective stocks as carefully as the geologist studies moon rocks, others hurl red darts at the **Wall Street Journal** and buy the pierced stock. Bankruptcy may fall to the former and success to the latter. The world isn't fair with reference to investors, political leaders, soldiers, and spouses. It is not fair that Robert Kennedy was assassinated and his eleven children will grow up without a father; it is not fair that Martin Luther King was killed because he was black; it is not fair for some boys to be drafted and, subsequently, shot in Vietnam, while others hide behind occupational deferments; it is not fair for some women to have retarded children.

Many people experience considerable unhappiness as a result of expecting the world always to give them a fair shake. It is helpful for both husbands and wives to realize that the world, in fact, is fair only sometimes (Madsen and Madsen, 1970). It is not fair that some husbands have had appropriate role models in terms of a mother and father who always responded in a positive way to each other, and that other husbands have had very negative role models where Mom and Dad rarely said a kind word to each other. Neither is it fair that some families will experience considerable financial difficulties, often involving bankruptcy, and others will never have a bill they can't pay. The productive couple will be aware that their happiness is not wholly dependent on external circumstances but on the specific behaviors which occur within their relationship. Marital partners have the choice to make each other happy and in these decisions they should disregard iniquities.

FUNCTIONAL DISCUSSION

A discussion is functional to the degree that the same problem does not recur. A husband and wife who discuss his being late do so in a meaningful and functional way if decisions are made which prevent the same problem from recurring. Recently, a wife indicated that she always became upset when her husband was late. The decision was made that the husband would call her within one hour after the designated time of his arrival if he would be more than one hour late. As an example, if he told his wife he would be home by nine o'clock, he would, in fact, be home by ten o'clock unless he called her between nine and ten and told her that he would be later than ten o'clock. To the degree that a discussion results in the nonrecurrence of the problem, the discussion has been functional. Behavioral decisions to implement new behaviors following a discussion contribute to marital happiness.

ON-TASK

Observational systems have been devised to assess the amount of time students spend "on-task" in the behavioral analysis of classroom behavior (Becker, Madsen, Arnold, and Thomas, 1967; Madsen, Becker, and Thomas, 1968). "On-task" behavior is defined as paying complete attention to the work or play situation or materials as prescribed within the classroom, and the absence of inappropriate behaviors which serve to get the child or his neighbors "off-task" (noises, hitting, staring into space, etc.). It is unfortunate that most married couples do not have the opportunity to have themselves observed by an independent, outside observer from the time they are together in the evening until just before bedtime. Most couples have very few set routines, and not only are they rarely giving their undivided attention to anything, but it also becomes exceedingly difficult to even imagine what they are supposed to be doing. Many, when confronted with observations from their homes, will reply that they value "flexibility." This begs the question.

As counselors, it is important to help couples make basic decisions about time use. "On-task" communication, for example, does not automatically occur just because two people are in the proximity of one another. Time must be scheduled which ideally has no interruptions. "On-task" communication does not occur in movie houses, while watching television, or necessarily, even when husband and wife take some time off and spend a week-end together. The counselor should schedule "on-task" time for spouses such as two fifteen-minute sessions daily. The partners then decide to turn off the television, put down the newspaper, etc., and communicate "on-task."

3. techniques

The relationship between the client(s) and the counselor is recognized as a crucial agent in achieving the goals of marital partners. The insensitive therapist will be ineffective regardless of his skill in applying various procedures. On the other hand, the therapeutic relationship should be supplemented by an array of procedures designed to influence human happiness.

Each of the following techniques has been detailed elsewhere (Ullmann and Krasner, 1965, 1969; Bandura, 1969; Franks, 1969). A brief overview is presented to acquaint the reader with how these techniques are utilized in dealing with marital problems. The creative therapist will perceive these techniques and their various applications as merely suggestive and will extend the range of techniques and modify their uses to meet the needs of his clients and patients.

SELECTIVE REINFORCEMENT

When any behavior (positive or negative) is followed by a desirable consequence, there is an increase in the probability that the behavior will recur. A behavior is strengthened when it is reinforced. Hence, to the degree that a response is rewarded, the response may be expected to recur. As an example, when a husband notices or gives attention to the fact that his wife has cleaned the house or apartment, he is increasing the probability of her housecleaning behavior. This is particularly true if he notices or gives attention to these behaviors every time they occur for the first few times. Afterwards, it is best to notice or give attention to these same behaviors only occasionally, since occasionally rewarded behavior tends to be maintained at a very high level.

Selective reinforcement is one of the most important learning principles in counseling and in life. The effective therapist will selectively reinforce positive, verbal, adaptive responses of his client, as will the client, through smiles, positive gestures, and verbal praise, reinforce the desirable behavior of his spouse. A wife who wants to increase the frequency of her husband calling her when he is going to be late is wise to thank him for calling when he does so. A husband who enjoys a particular meal which his wife has prepared should verbally and behaviorally reinforce the preparation of that meal.

It should also be understood that the husband or wife may inadvertently reinforce inappropriate or negative behaviors. As an example, the wife may say to her husband that she has noticed that he is beginning to spend more time at the office and that he always seems late in coming home. In effect, she is reinforcing both office and late behaviors by giving attention to each (rather than giving attention to staying home behavior). Since behavior is learned, it is important for the therapist and clients to be aware of what behavior is being taught.

EXTINCTION

Behavior that is maintained is being reinforced. Nagging, crying, yelling, being late, and forgetting are behaviors which are maintained by various reinforcing contingencies. A wife often continues to nag her husband because he has taught her if she will nag long enough, he will do what she has been asking. As an example, the wife who continues to tell her husband that the basement needs cleaning will usually be rewarded by her husband engaging in that behavior. Hence, he is teaching her that if she will nag him long enough about any specific behavior, he will perform that behavior.

Likewise, crying behavior is often maintained on the part of the wife by increased attention from the husband. In effect, the husband teaches his wife that if she will cry, he will give her his undivided attention, accompanied by expressions of love. In the same way, yelling behavior is often maintained because the person being yelled at will respond in the desired direction, thus teaching or reinforcing the person doing the yelling to continue.

Late behavior is often reinforced by considerable attention given to the partner who is late. The wife who is late is often the center of attention in that her husband will give her a prolonged dissertation on the merits of being on time, all of which may be extremely reinforcing to the wife. In addition, the wife will often teach her husband to forget by continually reminding him of a particular event. In effect, he learns that he has no need to remember because his wife will remember for him. It is clear that each of these behaviors is being maintained by an interpersonal reinforcer.

A goal of the client may be to extinguish or stop a specific behavior, such as nagging, crying, yelling, being late, or forgetting. To accomplish this, the specific reinforcer must be identified and withdrawn. If the reinforcer for each of the above behaviors is withdrawn, nagging, crying, yelling, being late, and forgetting will stop.

The withdrawal of a reinforcer must be consistent to be effective. As an example, if the husband is asked by his wife to wash the dishes, and he does so only occasionally, he is maintaining his wife's asking behavior at the very highest level. In order for him to extinguish her behavior of asking him to wash the dishes, he should never engage in that behavior. In this way, the wife learns that reinforcement does not follow this specific request. Of course, it is not important who washes dishes. It is important that the expectations of role performance are clear and contingencies established to maintain role behaviors and expectations.

Extinction is more efficacious when the incompatable behavior is rewarded. For example, while nagging (critical verbal remarks) is being extinguished, pleasant behavior (positive verbal remarks) should be observed and acknowledged. Similarly, while crying (frowning, tears) and yelling (loud verbal statements) behaviors are being extinguished, smiling and soft verbal behaviors should be reinforced. Finally, on-time and remembering behaviors should be rewarded while being late and forgetting behaviors are ignored. Spouses should always reward the behavior they want just as they ignore the undesirable behavior.

The counselor, too, may often choose to extinguish certain verbal behaviors of his clients. A client's discussion of only negative events during the counseling session will be extinguished by the therapist's non-attention or by a redirection of conversation. In effect, the therapist rewards the client through attention and verbal praise for engaging in behavior which is positive and goal directed, and does not reinforce negative, inappropriate behavior, nor that which is generally labeled as garbage behavior.

SYSTEMATIC DESENSITIZATION

Wolpe and Lazarus (1968), Lazarus and Serber (1968), Wolpe (1969), and D'Zurilla (1969) have discussed the procedures and uses of systematic desensitization. The format usually involves three stages: (1) listing a hierarchy of situations ranging from those which produce the least anxiety to those which produce the greatest anxiety, (2) training in relaxation which may be induced by hypnosis, a mixture of carbon dioxide-oxygen, or muscle tension release (see Appendix for relaxation instructions), and (3) the systematic pairing of the state of relaxation with the items of the hierarchy.

The basic premise of desensitization is that anxiety and relaxation are incompatible. When relaxation is substituted for tension, positive behavior becomes a more feasible possibility. The counselor will utilize this technique to reduce the anxiety of his client when faced with any particular problem situation. One of the most prevalent uses of desensitization is in the area of sexual behavior in which positive, appropriate sexual behavior tends to be inhibited by an undesirable increase in tension. In effect, desensitization assists the client in engaging in sexual behavior without anxiety.

A tape recorder is a useful asset in therapy in that the client can record the desensitization or relaxation session and play these tapes at home. This results in greater muscle relaxation and more speed of therapy.

IMPLOSION

Stampfl and Levis (1967) noted that the implosion of a particular negative thought often results in a more favorable attitude toward a specific situation. The client is encouraged to talk about things which bother him in a very extreme, unrealistic manner so that all possible negative alternatives are explored with the resulting realization that nothing drastic will happen. As an example, the wife confronted with the trauma of divorce is instructed to think in great detail about the specific effects of the divorce, such as increased loneliness, solitude, dependence on self, and separation from mate, to the extent that these thoughts lose their negative quality. In effect, the client becomes able to tolerate a degree of loneliness, looks forward to independence, and to the possibility of establishing other male relationships. However, there is also the possibility that the wife may become more anxious about the very event being imploded. For this reason, the writer has not used this procedure.

ASSERTIVE TRAINING

Salter (1961), Wolpe and Lazarus (1966), Wolpe (1969), Alberti and Emmons (1970), and McFall and Marsten (1970) have discussed the importance of assertive behavior. Anxiety is often a result of the unwillingness and/or inability to assert one's self. People who are often intimidated unreasonably do not assert themselves. This results in frustration, anxiety, guilt, and disappointment. The therapist, acting on the assumption that every person has worth and dignity and should be related to as a human being, will often train his clients to assert themselves and to insist on their legitimate rights as persons. A wife whose husband continues to have a mistress is taught to assert herself in terms of her expectations of him. Accordingly, when resentment is expressed, anxiety is decreased since the two emotions are often incompatible.

The ability to assert one's self is often dependent on a positive self concept. The term "self concept" as used here is an abstraction which refers to a variety of specific behaviors including self assertiveness. Husbands and wives who like themselves often feel free to communicate to the spouse their respective expectations. However, a good self concept may follow from training in assertive responses. Hence, the ability to assert one's self often results in a good self concept.

Through reasoning, assignment of tasks, and role playing, clients are reinforced for "asserting" themselves and developing the ability to insist on legitimate concerns. As an example, reasoning often involves a didactic interchange in which the futility of intimidation is explored. It is unreasonable for one human being to intimidate another for any reason; likewise, it is unreasonable for any human being to allow himself to be intimidated. Rather, the insistence on the part of the client that he be related to as a human being often prevents intimidation and provides a more cooperative relationship for the two people involved.

Assignment of tasks implies that the client will be assigned to engage in a repertoire of specific verbal responses when interacting with a specific individual. Males are often instructed to assert themselves with their friends, wives with their husbands, and coeds with their boyfriends. The counselor often models the role he believes his client should play. In the case of the woman whose husband continues to have a mistress, the counselor would play the role of the wife, while she plays the role of the husband. The counselor would then explain to the "husband" her willingness to change her behavior to make her husband happier. In return, she would expect her husband to terminate the relationship with his mistress. The wife then models after the counselor, while he plays the role of the husband. The same scene may be repeated a number of times until the client feels the role becomes her own. In effect, behavioral responses are systematically shaped so that the wife becomes comfortable in asserting herself to her husband and in making legitimate demands on him.

MODELING

Edgar A. Guest has written, "I can soon learn how to do it if you'll show me how it's done. Fine counsel is confusing, but example is always clear" (Guest, 1926). Modeling is valuable in that it provides a more positive array of behaviors which the client or couple can copy or imitate in their interactions with each other or with other people. The counselor will often model appropriate communication behaviors by responding positively to one of the partners and then having the spouse model after the counselor.

Favorable marital interaction may also be improved by having clients interact with people who exhibit desired responses (good model behavior). The couple is instructed to interact socially with friends who have a good marital relationship and who respond to each other in positive, appropriate ways. In viewing appropriate marital interaction, a generalization effect often occurs in which the partners begin to respond to each other in more adaptive ways.

Video tape is often a useful asset. A particular marital interaction sequence can be taped and played back with subsequent post-evaluation. In other words, the couples watch themselves and go over the problem again in an attempt to learn to respond in a more appropriate, productive way. This latter technique is most valuable for training couples how to communicate, discuss, compromise, and agree to disagree. For a systematic appraisal of the effects of modeling, Bandura and Walters (1963) and Bandura (1969) have provided an excellent discussion.

AVERSIVE CONSEQUENCES

Feldman (1966), Wilson and Davison (1969), and Rachman and Teasdale (1970) have discussed theoretical and practical issues of aversion therapy. There are various ways to use aversive consequences: (1) the presentation of aversive stimuli, and (2) the withdrawal of positive reinforcers. In the former situation, the counselor may use an electric generator to shock his client following mental images of behaviors the client would like to terminate. As an example, a husband is asked to think about approaching his secretary for a date and when this image is very clear, the therapist shocks him. The intent of this procedure is to make the thought of his secretary aversive. In addition, the counselor may discuss with the husband the negative consequences of continuing an affair, such as the loss of job, the loss of respect for self and wife, and moving from the community.

Often, the client is instructed to write down these aversive consequences, to carry these with him, and to read them when "flirting" behavior is likely to occur.

In utilizing the second type of aversive consequences, a wife may terminate intercourse if her husband does not blow in her ear while intercourse is occurring. Hence, a pleasant event, intercourse, is terminated following a specific, inappropriate behavior (cessation of blowing in ear). Covert sensitization, another aversive procedure, is discussed later.

STOP-THINK

This procedure involves the client interrupting his negative thoughts and substituting a more positive set of ideas (Wolpe and Lazarus, 1968). A female client recently noted that she felt extremely fearful of being home alone at night when her husband was out of town. The stop-think technique was used in that she was instructed to say to herself, "Stop" when she became aware of various ruminations concerning the possibility of someone breaking in the home and raping her. When she said "Stop," she was to get an index card out of her purse or drawer on which was written a number of pleasurable statements, i.e., she and her husband are very pleased with the recent grandchild, she and her husband will go to Miami for a vacation in the spring, their son is healthy and happy and has recently graduated with honors in a most promising field.

In effect, the negative pattern is being interrupted and substituted by thoughts incompatible with anxiety or unhappiness. This particular technique works well with most any type of mental compulsion in which the individual continues to ruminate about negative happenings. In effect, the cycle of these ruminations is broken.

PREMACK PRINCIPLE

The Premack principle (Premack, 1965) states that of any two responses, the more enjoyable one can be used to reinforce the less enjoyable one. In other words, if behavior A has a high probability of occurring and behavior B has a low probability of occurring, and if engaging in behavior A is made contingent on behavior B, there will be an increase in the probability of B's occurrence. This technique, including modifications and extensions by Homme (1965), Homme, et al. (1968), is frequently used to effect an attitude change. If the client wants to achieve a positive attitude toward the unenjoyable behavior, that behavior is made the stimulus for an enjoyable behavior. As an example, the husband who does not like to go

28

shopping with his wife, but who wants to achieve a positive attitude toward shopping, may make his job (behavior A) contingent on shopping (behavior B) with his wife. In one situation, a husband decided that he would work on his car (a high probability behavior) contingent on going shopping with his wife. Thus, he could earn time with his car by shopping with his wife. The result was a new, more adaptive, more positive attitude toward a previously negative event.

Mothers use this principle when they tell their children that they may have ice cream when they clean their plates. In essence, a high probability behavior (ice cream) is made contingent on a low probability behavior (finishing the meal). Parents make play time contingent on studying time, TV contingent on a clean bedroom, and time driving the car contingent on mowing the lawn.

The application of the Premack principle is a form of contingency contracting—one enjoyable behavior is made contingent on another behavior of the same person. A variation of contingency structuring involves engaging in a desirable activity contingent on the behavior of SOMEONE ELSE. The establishment of this contingency is designed to change the stimulus value of that person's (spouse's) behavior. As an example, a wife who does not like her husband to pilot small aircraft may make her enjoyable activities (shopping, calling "home," etc.) contingent on his flying. When her husband goes flying, she may then go shopping or engage in a behavior that she enjoys.

COVERT SENSITIZATION

Cautela (1966, 1967) discussed a technique whereby negative, noxious mental images are paired with undesirable behavior. As an example, in treating a man for alcohol approach behavior, Cautela would have the patient imagine a noxious smell which would result in vomiting over self and others at the time alcohol was imbibed. In this way, a negative association is established between the stimulus of drinking and the undesirable, noxious, negative results which follow.

COVERT REINFORCEMENT

Cautela (1970) also discussed a technique previously used by Homme (1965), D'Zurilla (1966), and Davison (1969) whereby clients may encourage positive changes in their behavior by the use of reinforcing thoughts. As an example, a husband who disliked his mother-in-law, but who valued a positive relationship with her, would think about the brim and bass he caught last week subsequent to his thought to visit his mother-in-law. In this way, a positive attitude toward visiting his mother-in-law may be effected. Initially, the client is trained to use this procedure in the counselor's office. After he becomes proficient in the self administration of mental reinforcement, he is instructed to use this procedure whenever maladaptive avoidance behavior and approach behavior occur.

COGNITIVE DISSONANCE

Festinger (1962) noted that the existence of dissonance (non-fitting relationships, inconsistencies in cognitions) is accompanied by an attempt on the part of an individual to reduce the dissonance, thus producing consonance (fitting relationships, consistency or harmony among cognitions). For example, a person who smokes heavily will avoid looking at TV advertisements about the harmful effects of smoking. The cognitive dissonance of smoking while watching a description of the lethal effects of smoking on the lungs can be reduced by changing stations or leaving the room.

Dissonance theory is utilized in marriage counseling by programming consonance through reading and essay writing. As an example, a devout Catholic who wants to alleviate her guilt over taking the pill may be instructed to write an essay on the merits of planned parenthood subsequent to a thorough investigation of the subject. Discussions about the essay and the importance of planning a family as well as statements regarding the undesirable aspects of unwanted children would be appropriately reinforced.

EXCHANGE CONTRACTS

Lederer and Jackson (1968), Stuart (1969), Rappaport and Harrell (1971), and Patterson and Weiss (Weiss, 1971) discussed the use of exchange contracts. Each spouse identifies behaviors he would like his partner to modify and agrees to modify his own behavior in exchange for the partner engaging in the desirable behavior. For example, a husband wanted his wife to wear a particularly attractive dress (increase wearing behavior of specified dress). His wife, on the other hand, wanted her husband to take her out to dinner (increase eating out together behavior). The contract established was as follows:

For Mrs. X.: I agree to wear the dress my husband finds attractive **if**, in return, he takes me out to dinner at a moderately priced restaurant within the next two weeks.

For Mr. X.: I agree to take my wife out to dinner at a moderately priced restaurant within the next two weeks **if**, in return, she wears a dress I find particularly attractive. (Rappaport and Harrell, 1971)

Weiss (1971) emphasized that rewards and penalties from the spouse, environment, and therapist should be specified to increase the probability of fulfilling the terms of the contract. For example, if a husband agreed to go to church with his wife, the contract would specify that he would be rewarded by (a) his wife helping him with his business records, (b) the privilege to fish the following Saturday, and (c) a reduction on his therapy bill by $5.00. However, failure to go to church with his wife would be penalized by (a) his sleeping on the sofa until the next Sunday, (b) loss of fishing privilege the following Saturday, and (c) an increase in his therapy bill by $5.00.

Stuart (1971) noted that exchange contracts should refer to increasing positive behavior rather than decreasing negative behavior. He further emphasized that each spouse should keep records on the desirable behaviors of his partner.

Potential strengths of behavior exchange contracts cited by Rappaport and Harrell (1971) include: (1) Teaches married couples reciprocal exchange and operant skills to help them resolve their present difficulties and those that will arise in their future; (2) Encourages couples to eliminate undesirable behaviors on a reciprocal basis and replace them with more desirable behaviors (those reinforcing to the marriage); and (3) Fosters self-reliance of the couple by having them negotiate their own behavioral-exchange contracts (with minimal dependence on the counselor).

Exchange contracts are one of the most effective and efficient procedures of the behavioral marriage counselor. By specifying what behaviors are to occur, when, with what consequences, marital happiness becomes a realistic possibility.

Each of the above techniques may be used alone or in combination. More important than "how," it is critical to discriminate what techniques (if any) should be applied to which problems manifested in which clients, when, and by what therapist. Behavior therapists sometimes may be too eager to use their plethora of techniques on problems of clients who don't want or need them. In some cases, the best "technique" may be to reassure the clients that their capacity to cope with their difficulty is quite adequate and that the therapist is available should they need additional assistance.

Some problems are not easily treated from a behavioral perspective. Spouses who are existentially confused about who they are or what they want may render the behavioral clinician helpless. Referral to a "traditional" or "gestalt" therapist may be in the spouses' best interests.

Spouses with the "same" problems may differ in their response to the "same" technique. Counselors should make calculated predictions of the efficacy of the possible application of various procedures to a specific client. As an example, desensitization may be the "treatment of choice" for a specific problem but not for a specific client who may have the problem.

The application of any procedure should usually be delayed until after a thorough assessment has been made and a "therapeutic relationship" developed. Although the distinction between assessment and therapy is never clear, initial procedures are generally applied between the first and third session.

Therapists differ in their competence and comfort with different clients and in applying specific procedures. All therapists are not suited for all clients. In some cases, referral may be the "technique of choice."

PART TWO

PART TWO

PROBLEMS IN MARRIAGE

Marital unhappiness may be defined as the absence of enjoyment in specific areas of marital interaction. Sex, communication, alcohol, in-laws, friends, religion, money, recreation, and children are alternative spheres of the conjugal relationship which frequently become barbed with discontent. The following procedures are suggestive of behavioral treatment which can be applied to specific marriage problems. These therapeutic behaviors may be helpful to the marriage counselor as he attempts to increase human happiness.

There is no behavioral recipe for marriage counseling. Each problem must be analyzed and treated individually. The innovative therapist will construct a specific treatment plan for his clients, as responsibility for appropriate modification lies with the counselor.

4. sex

Sex is one of the most frequent problems which occurs in marriage and in marriage counseling. The initial hesitancy in discussing sexual issues is avoided by having the clients complete the marriage inventory (see Appendix) in which they are requested to identify those problem areas (including sexual) they would like to deal with in therapy. Since our culture encourages people not to discuss sexual issues with strangers, the marriage inventory becomes particularly valuable.

The counselor may assist his clients in their discussion of sexual problems by discussing sexual issues himself in a calm, non-threatening, non-anxious manner. Some discussion of the meanings of sex and intercourse may be appropriate in providing this type of model. In essence, the counselor might indicate that:

> ...sex in human relationships implies more than intercourse. The word "sex" may refer to a wide range of behaviors such as exchanging glances, brushing elbows, holding hands, embracing, kissing, and intercourse. Sex can be thought of as a series of behaviors which may range from thoughts such as, "I like that person and want to touch that person," to an orgasmic experience during intercourse. A wife may say, "I hate sex," yet enjoy prolonged kisses of affection or being embraced by her husband.

> Just as sex may refer to different behaviors, intercourse may have different meanings. Intercourse may be referred to as orange juice, pie á la mode, cathedral, child, yoke, and shoe. Spouses may differ in the meaning they attach to intercourse at any particular time.

Orange juice intercourse is enjoyed for its tension-reducing properties. Just as orange juice contains vitamin C which is necessary for proper functioning of the body, intercourse might be desired because of the good feelings that it produces in the body. Orange juice intercourse results in a comfortable, relaxed, tension-free body that has enjoyed the experience of sexual union.

Pie á la mode intercourse is for fun. Just as riding a merry-go-round or ferris wheel, fishing, or sewing are enjoyable activities, intercourse may be enjoyed "just for fun," unrelated to its orange juice properties. Of course, intercourse for fun may also be intercourse for release, or vice versa.

Intercourse may also have a spiritual meaning. Cathedral (synagogue or church) intercourse is a union in which the "souls" of the partners touch in a type of mystical and spiritual experience. Cathedral intercourse results in the partner caressing the soul of the other in sexual union. Cathedral intercourse occurs within a strong bond of affection and love.

Child intercourse occurs only when children are the desired result. Although pleasure may occur, it is secondary to the hope of becoming pregnant. Some wives will submit to child intercourse only.

Yoke intercourse is that of obligation. Just as oxen bear the yoke of their master, so both husbands and wives may perceive intercourse as an obligation imposed on them by their spouse. Some husbands and wives have expressed the feeling that intercourse is something to be engaged in only at the mate's request. This results in a feeling of obligation, hence, yoke intercourse.

Shoe intercourse is the intercourse of habit. Some spouses have developed a sexual pattern whereby intercourse has become habitual, routine, and unenjoyable. It is analogous to putting on one's shoe; it is done out of habit.[1]

Clients readily identify the various meanings which they attach to intercourse, occasionally chuckle at their revelations, and frequently become more willing to verbalize their sexual concerns.

WHEN

Couples often disagree on when intercourse is to occur. The husband may begin to affectionately massage his wife just prior to supper in an attempt to get her stimulated for intercourse. At other times, the wife may choose to massage her husband in an erotic way while he is studying, talking on the phone, writing a letter, or repairing his fishing rod.

Other disagreements concerning the when of sex may be related to extremely early or late hours in which intercourse is desired by one of the partners. Some husbands enjoy coitus before breakfast, some at bedtime, and others during the night. Some women enjoy it at lunchtime, others only after a good movie, and still others after supper. Hence, the problem is that of disagreement over the time at which sexual behavior is to occur.

The treatment plan will vary from client to client, and couple to couple. However, a basic treatment plan is outlined below: The partners are asked to indicate the specific times they want sex to occur. In addition, they are to specify at what level they choose for sex to occur. As an example, the wife might be comfortable with caressing and fondling prior to supper, but not with intercourse. In the same way, the husband may enjoy affectionate kisses at noontime, but not intercourse.

If there is an agreeable time which the partners indicate that they would choose for sex to occur at a mutually understood level, this time would be identified as a sex time for the couple, and all the sex that they want on this level should occur within this specific time period. For example, if they both agree that intercourse prior to sleep is satisfying, the counselor would instruct them to engage in intercourse to satiation every

---

[1] Orange juice, pie á la mode, and cathedral intercourse are probably desirable and functional types of sexual interaction whereas child, yoke, and shoe intercourse are undesirable and dysfunctional meanings for intercourse. Treatment may involve a cognitive and/or behavioral shift from child, yoke, and/or shoe intercourse to some combination of orange juice, pie á la mode, and cathedral intercourse. (The concepts "orange juice intercourse" and "pie á la mode intercourse" were developed by Madsen, 1968.)

day at this particular time. Under these conditions, both partners will be attaining the needed quantity and quality and, at the same time, will provide enough satiation, each for the other, that the need for sex "between meals" will not be a problem.

If there is no agreement, the husband and wife should each specify the most desired time for something sexual. The husband may want intercourse following supper, whereas the wife may want it before sleep.

Positive, pleasurable activities for both husband and wife should be respectively identified. These are best identified by observing what the couple does. For example, if the husband fishes every weekend, this is a positive, pleasurable activity for him; if the wife sews a great deal, sewing is an enjoyable activity for her.

Each of these positive, pleasurable activities is placed on the Premack principle for sex. In other words, these enjoyable activities are made contingent on the participation in sex at a time desired by the partner. In this way, the husband's fishing trip would be contingent on having intercourse with his wife at bedtime, and the wife's sewing would be contingent on having intercourse with her husband after supper. Ostensibly, an agreement to alternate who can earn fishing and sewing privileges would be necessary so that sexual satiation does not occur.

Shortly after the desired level of sexual experience has occurred, the partner who, in the past, had not particularly enjoyed intercourse at that time would be given, by the spouse, a token which is symbolic of his or her earning the privilege to fish or sew the next day or weekend. Hence, the presentation of a rewarding token (stimulus) is to be made following the desired response. It is implied that each partner would, both verbally and nonverbally, reinforce his mate for engaging in sexual behavior.

Some clients may feel that this therapeutic approach is mechanical and cold in an area which is often surrounded by warmth and intimacy. Many clients become more willing to agree to the various rules when they are labeled as a "game" that, although unusual, does break undesirable habits and leads the way toward marital bliss. The Premack principle merely provides a more appropriate method of structuring the learning contingencies so that the desired behavior occurs. In this particular case, sexual behavior which occurs at a previously undesirable time would be reinforced by the privilege to engage in a specific enjoyable activity. In other words, intercourse at a particular time may be perceived as an opportunity to earn reinforcement elsewhere, rather than a responsibility or obligation to perform at a particular time.

FREQUENCY

Disagreement over frequency of intercourse is a recurrent sexual problem in marriage. It is usually the wife who complains that her beastly, insatiable husband "always has sex on his mind" (high rate of approach behavior), and the husband who complains that his wife sorely frustrates him by refusing him continually whenever he makes the slightest sexual approach (high rate of refusal behavior). Since behavior that is taught will be learned, in most situations, wives teach their husbands to approach at a very high level, as husbands teach their wives to refuse them at a very high level. In effect, wives maintain their husbands' high approach behavior by rewarding them occasionally. Hence, the husband learns if he continues to make sexual demands on his wife, sooner or later she is going to reward him. On the other hand, the husband is teaching his wife to refuse him since refusal is often accompanied by increased attention and prolonged solicitations for affection.

Frequency problems are often a result of a respective misunderstanding concerning the meaning of "sex" and "affection." Married men tend to lump affection and sex together, whereas women tend to separate them. Men who approach their wives for intercourse often feel that they are showing affection and hence, are often surprised when their wives accuse them of "never showing any affection." On the other hand, wives disconnect affection and sex by saying that they wish their husbands would give them more affection and less sex.

The treatment program for dealing with disagreements over frequency of intercourse will depend on how great the mutual desires are, and the history of the sexual conditioning of the spouses. (The counselor may need to deal with the latter issue independently.) In a typical situation, the husband will say that he would like intercourse at least four times per week, while the wife will indicate that she wants intercourse about once per week with interspersed periods of affection.

Assuming that the husband has the higher desire for frequency, the counselor should instruct the wife to approach her husband one more than the number of times he indicated was his desire for intercourse during a specific week. As an example, if the husband indicated that he wanted intercourse four times per week, the wife would be instructed by the counselor to approach him for intercourse five times during the next seven day period. In addition, the husband would be instructed to **refuse** his wife two or three of these five times. Refusal in this situation means a playful unwillingness to engage in intercourse and does not involve or imply rejection. As a result, the wife learns that her husband is not always ready for intercourse and is not the beastly, insatiable being which she anticipated since he has the capacity to refuse intercourse when it is available. In the same way, the husband learns that he need not be anxious about intercourse not occurring if his wife is going to approach him five times.

In addition, the husband is instructed to approach his wife every half hour he is in the house with her, put his arms around her, kiss her, tell her that he loves her, and never follow these behaviors with intercourse. In this way, his wife learns that affection is independent of intercourse and that his approaches to her, both verbally and physically, are behaviors for free and do not involve an attempt to obtain intercourse from her.

Another treatment alternative utilized in treating problems of frequency involves instructing the husband to approach his wife for intercourse at any time he desires, and for the wife to engage in foreplay for thirty minutes, after which time, if she so desires, she can refuse intercourse. Under these conditions, the ambiguities of sexual interaction are removed since the husband may always approach and his wife may always refuse after thirty minutes of foreplay. Both of these treatment approaches have been used with equal effectiveness.

HOW

Spouses may disagree on what behaviors constitute an enjoyable sexual experience. A wife may complain that her husband is very crude when he makes love. The counselor should ask that she define in more specific detail the behavioral referent of the word "crude" and specify what behaviors she regards as "gentle," "kind," "enjoyable," etc. In many situations, the husband is not aware that his behaviors are "crude" as defined by his wife, and often, being made aware of these behaviors, he will stop them. Other husbands begin "gentle" sexual behaviors only when contingencies are established.

Behavior that is maintained is rewarded. It is possible that the wife may be reinforcing the inappropriate or crude behavior of her husband by allowing him to continue to enjoy pleasurable sexual feelings in spite of his "crudeness." The counselor should suggest to the couple that the wife tell her husband what sexual behaviors she enjoys and make the continuation of sexual activity contingent on the husband's "gentle" behavior. The husband who squeezes the nipples of his wife too hard should not only be told that a soft, firm squeeze is desirable, but should be rewarded with kisses, and verbal praise for caressing the breast in the desired way. A gentle (or crude) husband or wife is taught to be that way.

Too little foreplay is a frequent complaint of the wife since the husband often penetrates before she is sexually excited and properly lubricated. The behavior of too little foreplay on the part of the husband is probably being maintained since the wife will usually submit to penetration regardless of the amount of time spent in foreplay. Treatment involves making the rule that the husband is to engage in thirty minutes of foreplay prior to penetration, and that the wife is not to submit to coitus prior to the half hour of foreplay she enjoys. In this way, the husband is reinforced for foreplay through the increased sexual excitement of his wife and a more active sexual partner during intercourse.

PREMATURE EJACULATION

One of the most frequent sexual problems encountered among husbands is premature ejaculation. Broadly defined, premature ejaculation is an unwanted ejaculation which occurs immediately before or after penetration. This uncontrollable, involuntary ejaculation (which usually results from excessive anxiety) causes embarrassment, feelings of inadequacy, and guilt in the husband, while the wife experiences frustration and often resentment toward her husband.

Since premature ejaculation is a behavior and hence, subject to various learning principles, a number of specific treatment techniques have been utilized, either alone or in combination. Before the application of any technique, information such as when, where, and how is obtained. As an example, does unwanted ejaculation occur frequently or rarely, depending on the time of day, the last ejaculation, position of intercourse, or the place of intercourse? Effective treatment should analyze the sexual response as it occurs in relation to the stimulus complex including the time, place, position, etc.

Although the specific treatment program will be dependent on the individuals involved (husband and wife) and the specific sexual response the husband makes, the general treatment plan is as follows: First, the client may be systematically desensitized to situations which result in anxiety for him. This involves three specific procedures: (1) during the latter part of the first session or the beginning of the second session where premature ejaculation has been identified as the specific problem to be dealt with, the client would be trained in deep muscle relaxation (see Appendix) so that he will be able to induce relaxation on his own; (2) the client is instructed to list a hierarchy of situations producing anxiety, beginning with that which involves the least anxiety and progressing to that which involves the greatest anxiety. As an example, most males indicate that they are extremely anxious immediately following penetration in that they fear ejaculation is imminent. This item would be the highest on the hierarchy. A very low item on the hierarchy would be shaving in the morning, a time in which absolutely no tension relative to sex is present. (3) after the client has been trained in deep muscle relaxation, systematic desensitization proceeds with the counselor requesting the client to imagine each of the scenes described in his hierarchy, while still relaxed, beginning with the scene which produces least anxiety and moving to those which involve more anxiety. As an example, for the first item presentation, the client would be instructed to think about shaving while still relaxed, and then move to the next item which may be taking a shower prior to bedtime. The basic premise of systematic desensitization is that anxiety and relaxation are incompatible behaviors and cannot, by definition, occur at the same time. If the client is relaxed, he cannot ejaculate prematurely.

Concurrent with desensitization or used exclusively, the client is instructed to be the aggressor in all sexual activity. The counselor explains to the wife that her husband is to initiate any sexual behavior that is to occur.

The reason for this procedure is that the aggressor frequently experiences less anxiety. Hence, if the client can control not only the initiation of sex, but also the level at which it occurs, his anxiety is likely to be reduced, and controlled ejaculation becomes a more feasible possibility.

A third basic procedure utilized to assist the client in maintaining a low level of tension is to have him perform only those sexual acts which he can enjoy without experiencing tension. The client is told to withdraw from any situation when a noticeable increment in anxiety occurs (Wolpe and Lazarus, 1968).

A male client noticed that sexual tension occurred while he was drying himself after having taken his shower. Tension occurred at this time due to his anticipation of intercourse which was to follow when he left the bathroom. Anxiety was reduced by getting back into the shower and by gradually moving from the bathroom into the bedroom. The client was withdrawing from a situation in which tension and anxiety existed for him. Later, he withdrew his penis while having intercourse so as to keep his tension level low. The result of his various withdrawals from situations of tension was his ability to maintain an erection and delay ejaculation for a prolonged period of time.

Other techniques which may be employed involve the application of a local anesthetic on the head of the penis to deaden sensation; instruction that the client is to perform either intercourse or masturbation three times daily for two weeks to decrease his sexual potency; counting while having intercourse to distract attention; or holding one's breath to displace sexual thoughts.

Although these latter techniques are suspect and probably only rarely assist the delay of ejaculation, Masters and Johnson (1970) have ably extended a useful technique developed by Dr. James Semans (1956). The wife manually manipulates the penis of her husband until he experiences the slightest feeling of impending ejaculation. At this time, she squeezes the head of her husband's penis between her thumb and two fingers. A three-to-four second squeeze will inhibit the desire to ejaculate. Manipulation is resumed after a thirty-second delay and the procedure repeated three or four times before ejaculation is allowed to occur. (During this phase of treatment, no intercourse is involved.)

After repeating this sequence on different occasions for several days or until sufficient control has been established, the treatment for ejaculatory delay during intromission begins. While the husband lies on his back, his wife straddles him and inserts his penis into her vagina. She sits slowly with no pelvic thrusting from either partner. Should the husband experience impending unwanted ejaculation, the wife would lift from his penis and apply the squeeze technique. After repeated trials, the husband is able to experience prolonged intromission without ejaculation. As he increases his ability to control ejaculation, pelvic thrusting is begun and other positions are adopted as desired. Masters and Johnson report 182 of 186 cases of premature ejaculation successfully treated—an impressive record.

IMPOTENCE

Impotence may be defined as the inability to create and maintain an erection. One of the first cognitions to be dealt with in treating impotence is to communicate to the husband that his penis is not under voluntary control, that he cannot voluntarily create an erection, because an erection is dependent on involuntary muscles. As an example, if someone were to place a German luger to the temple of a male and tell him that he must produce an erection within thirty seconds or he would be shot, the male would probably die.

The treatment of impotence usually involves a number of specific techniques which may be employed alone or in combination. Paradoxical intention (Frankl, 1960) is useful in creating a situation in which impotence does not occur. For example, the husband is instructed he is not to have intercourse under any circumstances, even though he may have a very stiff erection. The responsibility of achieving an erection being removed often results in the ability of the male to produce and maintain a sustained erection. In some cases, a client needs only a restructuring of the situation. If the use of paradoxical intention is successful, the client will return in two weeks saying that he "couldn't help it"; he had had such a good erection that he could not resist intercourse. In effect, he no longer has the problem of impotence.

A second strategy involved is that of teaching the male that there are any number of ways to satisfy his wife which do not involve the penis. Arnold Lazarus (1970) told the story of a male who indicated that he could satisfy any woman without taking his clothes off and without using his penis, and that this woman would return to him every time she wanted sex. Once the male can be convinced that there are any number of ways of satisfying his wife through the use of manual stimulation, cunnilingus, or through the use of an electric vibrator, the responsibility of using his penis is removed, and the onus of not being able to do so disappears. In order to affect this situation, the counselor will instruct the husband to satisfy his wife during the next week in a variety of ways, all of which do not include the penis. Normally, if this treatment approach is successful, he will return indicating that while satisfying her in other ways, his penis became very erect, and intercourse followed.

When a husband indicates there is considerable anxiety and tension associated with the thought of intercourse, particularly penetration, systematic desensitization is employed. The client is instructed to develop a hierarchy of sexual situations ranging from least to greatest anxiety, and is taught how to relax. Desensitization proceeds as the counselor presents the specific images to the relaxed client. Normally, when tension is the cause of impotence, desensitization will alleviate the problem although more sessions may be necessary.

Another technique involves the wife refusing the husband when he approaches her for intercourse. Among impotent males, there tends to be a history of females who are sexually aggressive and who encourage intercourse constantly. When the wife is instructed to turn her husband down every second time, the husband soon learns that his wife is not as desirous of intercourse as he had thought. Of course, it is important that the husband interpret his wife's refusals as her willingness to help him overcome his impotence rather than rejecting him as a person.

An additional technique involves the systematic building of successful erections. For example, the first time an erection occurs, the husband is instructed to maintain it for only a few seconds, and then allow it to subside. The second time he is to sustain an erection for an additional few seconds, working up to one-, two-, three-, four-, five-minute erections, each time. In effect, he learns a new attitude toward his erection. After a few seconds he has been successful in maintaining an erection, whereas, heretofore, he has been fearful of not being able to create and maintain any erection.

Each of these techniques has been successful in treating impotence. It will be necessary for the counselor to investigate the specific stimuli situations which result in impotence for the client and to utilize the technique which the therapist feels will be most effective for his client.

FRIGIDITY

Just as premature ejaculation and impotence are the predominant sexual complaints among husbands, so frigidity is one of the more frequent sexual complaints of wives. It is not unusual for a woman in therapy to sit almost motionless, and in a solemn, morose, tearful manner say that she does not enjoy intercourse with her husband and ask, "Is there anything to do?"

There is considerable disagreement over the definition of frigidity. Some authors define it as infrequent desire for sex; whereas, others might define it as clitoral orgasm only, as opposed to vaginal orgasm. (Masters and Johnson, 1966, emphatically state there are no physiological distinctions.) Frigidity as used here refers to little interest or enjoyment in sex. In essence, frigidity is a cultural label placed on the sexual response of women.

Although most males express very similar interpretations of their orgasmic experience, there is wide variability among females. Goldberg (1971) reported that some females were aware that an orgasm had occurred only in retrospect. They could not identify an "orgasm" while it was occurring.

Madsen (1968) discussed two types of orgasmic responses which women subjectively report. These may be defined in terms of a violin or crescendo orgasm. The violin orgasm is characterized by pleasurable sexual feelings which occur following stimulation but does not involve a peak period or a period significantly different from a general level of sexual excitement. It is like the music of a single violin, which is soft and beautiful, and when over, has been pleasant.

On the other hand, the crescendo orgasm involves an intense, identifiable peak experience which occurs during sexual excitation. Intense breathing, screams, and a quivering body are often characteristic of a crescendo orgasm. It should be understood that women vary greatly in their capacity to respond to sexual stimuli and that variations in sexual response do occur. Thus, there are any number of women who experience the violin type of orgasm, but do not experience the crescendo type of orgasm and vice versa.

The treatment for the inability to respond favorably and positively to sexual stimuli should begin with a complete medical examination to ascertain the presence of any physical dysfunctions. It is not unusual for a counselor to spend months in therapy with a "frigid" woman only to discover that her pain during intercourse is the result of a uterine infection and/or inflammation. Assuming that the woman's physician has obviated medical etiology, therapy may involve the following procedures: (1) reading of sexual materials, (2) sensate focus,

(3) desensitization, (4) artificial stimulation, (5) sexual experimentation, and (6) frequent sexual behavior. These procedures may be used alone or in combination.

The woman who responds slowly or negatively to sexual stimuli usually has had very little sexual information available to her in the past. When available, it was probably negative. As an example, mothers often teach their daughters that sex is an obligation of the wife and is not to be enjoyed. **Human Sexuality** (McCary, 1967) and **The Sensuous Woman** (J, 1969) are suggested to the wife to read as a basis for developing accurate information and loosening her cognitions about sex. Frequently the counselor will discuss specific topics which were of interest to the client in an attempt to clarify points of misinformation and get the wife to verbalize her feelings about sex.

Consistent with learning more accurate information about sex, the wife is encouraged to experience pleasurable sexual sensations without feeling obligated to have intercourse. To accomplish this experience, Masters and Johnson (1970) developed what they referred to as "sensate focus." The experience assumes that touch is an important element in human personal communication that gives meaning to sexual responsiveness for the spouses. The procedure as related to the treatment of frigidity involves the partners lying nude together while the husband explores touching his wife's body who gives him direct feedback about what she feels. Initially, manipulation of the genitals and her breasts are avoided. The result of this procedure allows the wife to attend to the pleasure her body is capable of experiencing without feeling pressured to have intercourse.

For wives who are particularly fearful of sexual contact, systematic desensitization may be necessary. The wife is instructed how to relax and is told to practice these relaxation sessions during the next two weeks at least twice a day. In addition, a hierarchy of sexual stimuli is drawn up. Frequently, these are put on index cards and arranged in a hierarchal sequence from those items which cause the least anxiety to those which cause the greatest anxiety. As an example, the item of greatest anxiety may be her husband pushing his penis far into the vagina, whereas an item very low on the hierarchy might be her putting on her pajamas and preparing for bed.

After the client has learned how to relax and a hierarchy has been constructed, desensitization proceeds with the counselor having the wife think about each of the items on the hierarchy while still relaxed so as to pair relaxation with each of these particular items. Again, the premise of desensitization is that anxiety and relaxation cannot occur at the same time. If the wife is relaxed when she is thinking about these various sexual scenes, she cannot, by definition, be anxious.

Brady (1966) described a modification of the desensitization procedure by inducing relaxation using intravenous methohexital sodium (Brevital). The procedure obviates preliminary training in relaxation and hastens desensitization.

Madsen and Ullmann (1967) demonstrated the effectiveness of using husbands in the counseling session to assist the wife in visualizing different sexual activities. The husband is instructed by the counselor to read aloud a particular item which his wife has previously written on an index card and, in a sense, verbally seduce her in the same way he would were they home. This procedure is valuable since it helps to generalize a positive effect of desensitization from the office to the bedroom.

Desensitization is used to reduce anxiety which inhibits sexual contact. Where anxiety is minimal, the electric vibrator (see Appendix), an unconditioned stimulus, is useful in the treatment of frigidity. When properly used, it will result in a pleasurable orgasmic experience for the wife.

Some wives express that they are unwilling to use a machine to achieve an orgasm. The therapist may suggest that the vibrator is a means of assessing the wife's capacity for orgasmic response and note that the vibrator is one means of achieving sexual satisfaction—as is intercourse, cunnilingus, manual stimulation by the husband, and masturbation. There is a vast range of sexual behaviors which will produce pleasurable, positive sensations in the wife, the vibrator being a more powerful force to create the experience of orgasm.

After the wife has read considerably in the area of sex, reports little anxiety anticipating or during sexual contact, and has utilized the electric vibrator to achieve positive, pleasurable sexual sensations, she and her husband are instructed to experiment together in an attempt to find out what specific sexual behaviors result in the greatest pleasurable feelings for her. As an example, some women experience their most pleasurable sexual feelings when intercourse is preceded by manual stimulation on the part of the husband. It is these types of behavioral repertoires that the wife should begin to identify and to engage in frequently.

Frequency of sexual excitation is necessary in the treatment of problems such as "frigidity," "no orgasm," or "little interest in sex." Hence, the wife is instructed to engage in a behavioral repertoire of sex several times each week so that her body becomes accustomed to responding in a very pleasurable sexual way. Again, the wife may act herself into a new way of thinking about sex by engaging in frequent, pleasurable sexual activities.

Wives who are unwilling to cooperate in the treatment program such as reading about sex, experiencing sensate focus, participating in desensitization (where necessary), etc. are referred to other therapists on the premise that pleasurable sexual experiences will best occur through the changing of their sexual behaviors rather than through extensive therapeutic discussions of why they do not enjoy sex.

INFIDELITY

Infidelity is not a new phenomenon in marriage. Kinsey (1948, 1953) indicated that one-half of all married males and one-fourth of all married females have extra-marital relations at least once during their marriage. Hence, affairs tend to be one of the more common problems encountered by marriage counselors.

The involvement of a spouse in an extra-marital affair is the result of: (1) an inability or unwillingness on the part of the individual to decide on his or her hierarchy of values relative to people, and (2) an inability or unwillingness to discriminate between thought and behavior. A relationship between a spouse and another party will develop in a positive direction if a number of favorable events occur over a period of time. Any two people who log a considerable amount of positive time together will tend to have a favorable attitude toward each other. This is particularly true when a spouse is unhappy and is spending time with a third party. A man or woman who chooses to spend his or her time heterosexually to the exclusion of the spouse is making a decision of valuing one person over another. There are many husbands who insist they love their wives very much, yet they choose to spend their vacations with their secretaries, and many wives who say that they love their husbands very much, but they choose to spend the week-end at the beach with the next door neighbor.

Affairs also result from an inability to discriminate between positive thoughts and objective behaviors. Every person feels positive about people other than his or her spouse, e.g., husbands appreciate secretaries who do good work and wives like the kind salesmen at the appliance store. Infidelity begins when a discrimination between the enjoyment of a positive, favorable feeling toward another leaves one's thoughts and enters one's behavior. As an example, a husband who may feel very positive about his secretary is still being honest with himself and his wife as long as he does not attempt to meet her after hours or become physically involved with her.

There are basically three problems relative to infidelity which occur in marriage counseling: (1) the husband or wife is ambivalent about whether to terminate the relationship with the spouse or lover, (2) the husband or wife chooses the spouse, (3) the husband or wife chooses the lover.

In the situation in which the client is ambivalent about whether to terminate the relationship with the spouse or lover, the counselor must first ascertain from him a willingness to decide to decide. In essence, a decision must be made to terminate one relationship and strengthen the other. The necessity for such a decision assumes that the spouse or mistress is unwilling to share the husband. Secondly, the counselor should explore with the client the consequences of his decision. As an example, for a man to decide that he will end his marriage, the consequences of alimony, loss of job, withdrawal from children, and his "self-concept" are explored. On the other hand, should the husband decide to terminate the relationship with his mistress, the consequences of her resentment, the termination of an enjoyable relationship forever, and the void which will result because of the needs which she was fulfilling must be evaluated. Questions which have been helpful in assisting a husband in reaching a decision include: (1) If you had two tickets to the Rose Bowl game and you could take only one woman, whom would you choose? (2) Which woman has more of the qualities which you would want your daughter to possess? (3) If your son came to you asking you which woman he should marry, whom would you advise him to marry? It is clear that these questions focus on the values of the spouse involved.

A second problem in the area of infidelity occurs when the husband or wife chooses to live with the spouse. Treatment proceeds from this point, which is basically two-pronged:

A. The counselor will assist the spouse in withdrawing from the lover or mistress by programming a number of specific behaviors. As an example, in the case of the husband who is terminating the relationship with his secretary, he is instructed to write her a letter telling her: (1) he chooses to withdraw from the relationship with her completely, and forever, (2) he chooses to interact with her now on a Mr. and Miss basis only and will not respond otherwise under other conditions, (3) she is not to touch him or to respond to him as she has previously done, since he has decided to improve his marriage, (4) he does not intend to see her under any conditions other than those which the work involves, and (5) if possible, she is informed that her desk is being moved out of visibility from his office. In essence, the relationship is so structured that an affair cannot continue since an affair is dependent on the continuation of positive responses of one to the other.

B. In conjunction with assisting the client in the termination of the relationship with his mistress or lover, the specific behaviors of the spouse that are unpleasant and which need to be changed become the focus of treatment. In other words, the spouse has been engaging in behaviors which do not result in happiness for the straying spouse. Hence, the focus of counseling becomes improving the behaviors in the relationship with the spouse so that the relationship becomes more reinforcing or rewarding. In some situations, the husband who has decided to recreate the relationship with his wife is instructed to take his wife to a motel, out to eat, and on short vacations to re-establish the romantic air of marriage.

A third problem encountered in the area of infidelity involves the husband or wife choosing the mistress or lover. When this occurs, the counselor focuses on assisting the remaining spouse in readjusting to the actions of the partner. Once a decision has been made to leave the spouse, the counselor forces this issue by having the spouse call a lawyer while in the office to make an appointment to draw up the separation and divorce papers that afternoon or the following day. The assumption is made that if the relationship is going to be severed, more pain, frustration, worry, guilt, and disappointment result from a continuation of the ambivalence. To reiterate, the counselor would meet with the remaining spouse to assist him or her in establishing alternative life goals and in learning to live without the spouse.

One technique utilized to assist a spouse in getting over a broken relationship is to have the husband or wife write down all the bad things which have occurred in the marriage, and to read this list systematically when he or she is thinking about the positive things of the past relationship. Many wives keep terminated relationships vividly alive by remembering positive events, which results in a very morose, tearful, solemn, and sad existence. The counselor forces the remaining spouse to think about the relationship in a very realistic way. The wife is forced to realize that her husband loved her so much that he lied to her, slept with another woman, and left her. Usually after a woman can conjure up a good image of her husband sleeping with his mistress, her positive affect dwindles sharply.

The systematic application of therapeutic procedures to sexual problems should follow a decision by both partners to work toward desired changes. Until such a commitment by the spouses has been made to ameliorate specific problems, therapy will be pointless. Once values are clarified and decisions made, the therapist and spouses collaborate to determine the most efficient and acceptable plan of treatment.

Resistances do occur. Just as some wives explain that they "cannot" use the vibrator to overcome lack of enjoyment in sex, husbands often refuse to withdraw from sexual excitation to inhibit impotence. Clients sometimes cannot envision themselves continuing the sexual behaviors outlined in therapy forever. To overcome this, the therapist explains that the treatment behaviors are "timebound," with six weeks often being chosen as the length of the treatment. At the end of six weeks, many sexual problems will have been alleviated. In other cases, significant improvement will have occurred which usually results in enough encouragement to bid for additional time if needed.

Sex is one of the most important ingredients in an enjoyable relationship. Couples plagued with sexual disagreements, misunderstandings, and dysfunctions are often robbed of the potential to achieve marital ecstasy. Through new adaptive sexual behavior, mutual sexual fulfillment results and enhances the experience of marriage happiness.

5. communication

Lack of adaptive communication is a major problem in an unhappy marriage. Likewise, it is one of the more frequent problems encountered in marriage counseling. Marriage counselors are aware of the number of spouses who do not have the skills required to communicate effectively with each other.

Since psychotherapy can probably best be described as a learning experience, the counselor may often increase the speed of therapy by teaching his clients basic issues about communication. Communication refers to a message which is transmitted through both verbal and nonverbal behavior. Verbal behavior refers to literal content. A wife who says to her husband, "I don't mind if you go bowling tonight," is saying to her husband, in words, that she has a positive or at least neutral attitude toward her husband's being away that evening. Nonverbal behavior refers to the gestures, facial expressions, and tone of voice, which communicate a context within which the verbal content is to be understood. The wife, with tears in her eyes, a disappointed tone, a droopy facial expression, and a listless gesture, who says that she does not mind if her husband goes bowling, in effect, is indicating behaviorally very clearly that she does.

The counselor should notice the verbal and nonverbal behavior of his clients as they interact during the counseling session, and note when discrepancies occur. It is not unusual that a double message is sent by a spouse as illustrated with the example above. Adaptive communication requires that the two levels be congruent, so that one message is communicated (Satir, 1967). For example, if a wife is comfortable about her husband's going bowling and they decide this is an appropriate behavior, she will communicate her approval not only in words, but also through her facial expression, tone of voice, eyes, gestures, etc. Implicit in the notion of the respective levels of communication is the idea that something is always communicated, either through words or behaviors. When a husband and wife are together, it is impossible for them not to communicate something, each to the other. Just as there are respective levels and ways of communication, there are discrepancies in the sending and receiving of messages. It is crucial that the husband and wife be aware that the messages that they send are the same messages that the spouse receives. Questions asked by the respective partners which assist them in understanding the meaning communicated include: "Do you mean ---?" "What exactly do you mean?" and "What does 'that' refer to?" Hence, the message sent is brought into line with the message received.

Madsen (1968) developed four critical issues of marital communication: honest, dishonest, direct, and indirect questions. An honest question is one in which the respondent can respond negatively without penalty. If the husband asks his wife an honest question, he will not get angry at her response. In effect, he wants to know what his wife thinks. The husband who asks his wife, "Do you want to have intercourse tonight?" is asking her an honest question if she can say, "No," without his getting angry. A wife who asks her husband if he would like to visit her relatives is asking an honest question if he can say, "No," without her getting angry.

A dishonest question is one in which the respondent cannot respond negatively without penalty. If the husband becomes angered when his wife responds, "No, I would not like to have intercourse," a dishonest question has been asked. If the wife becomes saddened at her husband's response, "No, I would not like to visit your relatives," the question was dishonest. Couples are assisted in asking honest questions by: (1) deciding if their questions are honest and (2) asking the mate if he is asking an honest question. The wife who is asked by her husband, "Do you want to have intercourse?" should verify her husband's honesty.

Honest questions are important since they keep the partners communicating in a candid way with each other, while dishonest questions make it clear who has the problem. For example, if a husband becomes angry at his wife's refusal to have intercourse with him, he has asked a dishonest question, and, therefore, he has the problem.

Dishonest questions are not limited to marriage partners. Everyone has been asked dishonest questions such as, "Are you busy?" "Do you mind if we pay you later?" or "Am I in your way?"

Asking a direct question is as important as asking an honest question. A direct question asks specifically what you want to know. "Do you want to have intercourse?" is a direct question, whereas, "Are you tired tonight?" is an indirect question if intercourse is desired. Wives sometimes ask their husbands, "How do you like my new dress?" (indirect question) when they may want to know how appealing they look. Boys sometimes ask their dates, "What time do you have to be in?" (indirect question), when they may want to know if their date wants to make love. Hence, direct questions ask for specific information desired, and indirect questions are a subtle way of ascertaining the information which could be obtained by asking direct questions.

Concerning honest and direct questions, an honest question is always a direct question. As an example, if a husband asks his wife an honest question, "Are you tired tonight?" and she says, "Yes," he will not get angry. In the same way, it was a direct question if he did not mean, "Do you want to have intercourse?"

A dishonest question may be both a direct question and an indirect question. A boy may ask his date, "What time do you have to be in?" and be asking specifically for that information. On the other hand, he may ask, "Are you tired tonight?" which would not only be a dishonest question if he does not care whether she is tired, but also an indirect question if he wants to know whether she would like to make love.

It follows that a direct question is not necessarily always an honest question. The boy who asks, "Do you want to make love?" is asking exactly what he wants to know, yet the question is not honest if he becomes angry when she says, "No." However, there are situations in which the direct question may be honest. For example, a boy may really want to know if his date wants to make love and will not get mad if she says no. (See Figure 1.)

TOO LITTLE COMMUNICATION

Many couples who seek marriage counseling spend only a small amount of time together. A helpful technique is to schedule "talk time" in which the couple is instructed to engage in on-task communication (television off, phone off hook, children in bed, dog fed, newspaper down, etc.) twice a day for two fifteen-minute periods. Initially, the interaction is structured by the counselor. The husband asks the wife questions relative to what she did during the day, and the wife asks about things of specific concern to her husband. In addition, some time is spent talking about a mutual interest they either have or intend to develop.

A record is kept of the amount of time spent talking and brought to the next counseling session. This record not only assists the counselor in being aware of what his clients are doing outside the interview, but also provides the clients an external stimulus and reinforcement for spending time together.

INTERESTS DIFFER

Differential interests of husband and wife are not unusual. This is particularly true when the husband is involved in a profession which demands a specific type of knowledge of which the partner would not be

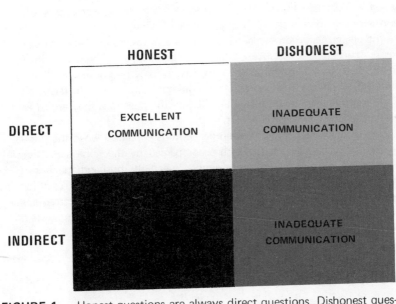

FIGURE 1   Honest questions are always direct questions. Dishonest questions may be direct or indirect. Direct questions may be honest or dishonest, whereas indirect questions are always dishonest. Good communication requires that questions be both honest and direct.

aware unless she were in the same profession. On the other hand, many wives learn skills, such as ceramics, sewing, rug making, or cake baking, which have a specific jargon of which the husband is not aware. A technique utilized to assist couples who have differential interests is to have the respective partners read so many pages each day in the area of interest of their spouse and discuss what they read with the spouse. In one situation, a wife whose husband had a Ph.D. in sociology was instructed to read an article a day in one of his professional journals and discuss this article with her husband during their "talk time." In essence, the wife became more interested in what her husband was doing, and he became more interested in her as a result of her ability and willingness to communicate about something which became a mutual interest.

SEXUAL COMMUNICATION

Couples frequently are unable to discuss sexual interests or phenomena with each other and may feel that this is a forbidden area of discussion. A technique to assist these couples in achieving a less hesitant attitude toward discussing sex is to have them write down, independently, all the sexual words they know. They then say each of these words, one after another, together until the verbalization of these previously forbidden words elicits no negative reaction. This usually results in a willingness to discuss particular sexual issues which may be of value to them, but which, in the past, they had hesitated to do because they had been unwilling to say the specific sexual words. If a communication block persists, the counselor may provide the clients with specific questions they are to ask each other to open these channels.

Sexual communication generally is enhanced when the rule is made that each touch should be accompanied by the honest question, "How does that feel?" As an example, when the husband touches his wife's breast, he is to ask her how that feels, and request her to tell him what is most pleasurable for her. Often, the touch-and-ask rule results in more sexual pleasure for the husband and wife as each becomes aware of what is most pleasurable to the spouse.

KIND COMMUNICATION

A client recently indicated that he wanted nothing more from therapy than for his wife to communicate with him in a very kind way. Although it was very difficult for him to identify specific behaviors which he labeled as being "kind," the decision was made that he would carry poker chips in his pocket and give one of these to his wife every time she exhibited a "kind" behavior. In effect, he was selectively and positively reinforcing behaviors which he defined as being "kind," behaviors which he chose to increase, and which subsequently did. Coupled with the program was the loss of five chips following the occurrence of "unkind" behavior. (Each poker chip was worth two dollars which she could spend as she chose.)

It is this type of behavioral technique which quickly improves behaviors in marriage. Systematic reinforcement for desirable behaviors and punishment for undesirable behaviors result in a quick cessation of that which is not desired and a considerable increase in that which is.

ARGUMENTS

Arguments are defined as verbal behaviors which are loud, while discussions are soft verbal behaviors. For some couples, it is unwise for them to continue to argue since very little is resolved. For others, discussions are very functional since they result in a plan to prevent the same problem from occurring again. A technique frequently utilized to stop arguments is to have the partner who is least likely to "get hot" say to the spouse, "You're getting angry," at which time the partner should withdraw from the room and stay for a period of several minutes until he or she is able to return without considerable emotion.

Another technique helpful in improving marital communication is modeling, which is often accomplished by a spouse interacting with the counselor in a positive way. In effect, a positive model of marital communication is provided for the spouse, who then practices communicating with the mate while the counselor observes and reinforces positive behaviors of communication. Clients are also instructed to interact socially with happily married couples, thus providing other more adaptive, more appropriate, positive models within their social context.

It is often desirable to limit the discussion of certain "dangerous" topics until they have first been discussed in the presence of the counselor. During sessions acceptable topics are outlined and the couple limit communication to those topics during the scheduled "talk-time." Later, following appropriate practice, new topics which previously resulted in arguments are introduced one at a time.

LOVE

A marriage without love is like a flower without fragrance, algebra without symbols, and India without cows. Spouses often desire to recapture the love feelings they experienced during courtship. Duplications of these feelings are rarely a possibility since courtship love attitudes can only occur during courtship. However, romantic attitudes toward love have been observed among different populations including couples married over twenty years (Knox, 1968; 1970).

Two procedures may be implemented to assist couples in developing the love feelings they desire. First, an examination of the love concepts of the respective spouses may result in altering dysfunctional attitudes. Although the counselor might best use his own skill in discussing various love phenomena, a discussion guide may be helpful (Knox, 1971).

In addition to the cognitive procedure, behavioral indices of love feelings should be ascertained. The husband or wife should be asked to identify what specific behaviors of the spouse are interpreted as meaning that the partner is loved. Responses vary. Some wives feel that they are loved when their husband comes home early for supper rather than delaying at the tavern or pub. Husbands often note that their wives love them when they cook good food, keep a clean house, and enjoy intercourse. Therapy should focus on setting contingencies to develop the desired behavior.

A behavioral approach to marital communication implies a concern for the content and means (verbal and non-verbal) of communication. Communication patterns are learned. It is the therapist's responsibility to structure new learning experiences to effect more adaptive communication. In this way, spouses may not only experience increased happiness but will be able to express these feelings more clearly.

6. alcohol

The use of alcohol is a frequent problem encountered in marriage and in marriage counseling. Alcohol becomes a problem when it interferes with the positive, adaptive functioning of the individual in any area of his life (Middleton, 1968). When a man's drinking interferes with his job performance, his marriage, or his "self-concept" (approving cognitions about himself), drinking has become a problem. Many clients deceive themselves when they contend that drinking is not a problem, although there is an obvious interference and disruption in the functioning of their lives. Indeed, the first goal of therapy may involve assisting the clients in recognizing the negative consequences, both individual and marital, of the excessive use of alcohol.

WHO DRINKS

Spouses may disagree over the appropriateness of drinking alcohol. In many cases, either the husband or wife enjoys drinking, but the spouse disapproves. Where the wife wants her husband to drink "moderately," the counselor should define "moderately" (two ounces of hard liquor per twenty-four-hour period) and ask the husband what behaviors he would like his wife to increase. Examples of frequent behavioral requests which husbands make include, "Serve dinner on time (7:00 p.m.)"; "Keep the living room clean (papers off floor, furniture dusted, T.V. Guide on table next to chair)"; and "Approach me for intercourse occasionally (once each week)."

The respective behavioral requests are "traded off" in a contractual agreement. For example, the husband agrees to restrict his daily drinking to the specified amount of alcohol in return for his wife serving dinner, keeping living room clean, and approaching him for intercourse (weekly). Each spouse records the positive behaviors of the partner and brings the records to therapy.

Even though the wife has agreed to her husband's drinking a prescribed amount, she may still feel anxious and negative about his doing so. Other procedures may be used to assist her in becoming more tolerant of alcohol. Systematic desensitization may be employed in an attempt to reduce her anxiety when her husband imbibes. The result of such a procedure allows the husband to drink in the home, in the presence of his wife, without initiating negative verbal response from her and without increasing her anxiety.

Another technique to increase the tolerance of the wife toward her husband's drinking alcohol involves having her drink all of her liquids out of a container from which her husband usually drinks his booze. If the husband usually drinks Budweiser beer, the wife is instructed to obtain an empty Budweiser can, cut out the top of the can, and drink her water, orange juice, tea, coffee, and milk from this container. Clearly, this is an effort to change the stimulus value of the Budweiser beer can by associating it with more pleasurable, primary reinforcers.

Modeling may be employed in that the counselor will ask the client to socialize with people whom she values a great deal and who drink beer or liquor. In this way, a positive modeling experience may occur for the client.

A fourth technique involves establishing a contingency so that enjoyable behaviors of the wife, such as cooking, walking the baby, reading the newspaper, watching television, sewing, etc., are made contingent on the lack of negative statements to the husband when the husband drinks a previously agreed amount (two ounces of hard liquor per day). The wife earns the privilege to engage in the behaviors which she enjoys when no "nagging" follows the husband's drinking only the specified amount.

Although each of the above procedures may be useful in increasing the wife's tolerance toward her husband's drinking, there are obvious difficulties. In desensitization, the wife may not be able to proceed far enough along her hierarchy before her husband begins to control his drinking (which he may never do). Hence, the husband's continued excessive drinking could exacerbate her negative reactions (physiological and overt) and obviate successful desensitization.

In regard to changing the stimulus value of the Budweiser beer can, it can be argued that the negative "meaning" of the alcohol is avoided. It is probably true that exploring the wife's cognitions about alcohol and using Ellis's rational emotive therapy would be productive therapeutic avenues which may induce more permanent changes.

Although the modeling procedure may be useful in developing a more positive orientation to alcohol, it may be impractical since few "teetotalers" socialize with friends who drink. The Premack principle contingency probably has the greatest potential for decreasing nagging behavior and was successfully employed in one case where the husband also selectively reinforced his wife for the appropriate behavior.

Although the wife usually complains about her husband's drinking, it is not unusual for the husband to feel that his wife should not drink. In dealing with this situation, the same procedure of having the spouses "trade off" respective behavioral requests in a contract is utilized. If the husband appears to be more tolerant toward his wife's drinking than she is tolerant toward not drinking, an attempt is made to increase his tolerance utilizing the techniques mentioned above.

HOW MUCH

It is not unusual for a spouse to decide to control his drinking. A male client with a history of chronic drinking had been told by his doctor that he must drink moderately if he chose to live. A number of procedures were established to assist him in controlling his drinking: (1) an acceptable limit of drinking was established—one beer or one jigger of liquor per day. The rule was made that should the husband drink more than the prescribed amount, his wife would call the sheriff in the community, and the husband would be jailed for forty-eight hours. This agreement was written in the form of a contract, signed by the client, the sheriff, and the counselor. (2) Each day the husband controlled his drinking, his wife was to reward him one point which would be recorded on a calendar hanging in the kitchen and say she was proud of him. These points were traded for his wife accompanying him on a fishing trip, since the client had indicated that one of the "great joys of life" was for his wife to go fishing with him. The above program resulted in initial failure because of the sheriff's unwillingness to jail the client, although he had agreed to do so. In effect, the sheriff said that he did not want to lock up his friend. A telephone call to the sheriff reiterated the importance of incarcerating the client upon violation of his part of the agreement. The sheriff acknowledged his participation in the contract and agreed to jail the client for subsequent violations. Therapy was terminated because the counselor moved out of the city. A three-year follow-up with the wife indicated that the husband had resumed his excessive drinking. However, no contingencies had been applied to his drinking behavior since therapy was terminated.

Aversion therapy may be useful in the treatment of undesirable drinking behavior. This includes the use of electric shock and aversive mental images. One procedure, utilizing electric shock, (Blake, 1965) involves shocking the client as he sips his favorite drink with the shock being terminated contingent on spitting out the drink. Another variation may involve having the client verbalize a clear mental image of his behaviors prior to and during drinking episodes, such as ordering a beer at a tavern, putting the mug to his lips, or reaching for a six pack of beer at the grocery store. While the client verbalizes these thoughts, the therapist yells "Stop," and shocks the forearm of the client. The shock is terminated when the client verbalizes a new thought pattern, e.g., orders a Coke at the tavern, puts the mug down and leaves, or reaches for Pepsi Cola instead of Pabst Blue Ribbon at the grocery store.

Lovibond and Caddy (1970) utilized a technique designed to train the alcoholic to become a moderate, controlled drinker by teaching him to discriminate his own blood alcohol concentration. This procedure involved shocking the patient when his BAC was elevated above an established criterion.

Mills, Sobell, and Schaefer (1971) contingently shocked male alcoholics for exhibiting drinking habits typical of alcoholics (drinking straight liquor in large gulps and large amounts). Although no generalization or follow-up data are available, all of the 13 hospitalized patients learned the behavior characteristic of a social drinker within 14 sessions.

Disulfiram (antabuse) may be useful when prescribed and supervised by a physician. However, Lubetkin, Rivers, and Rosenberg (1971) noted the difficulty in getting patients to take the drug routinely and suggested the need for an inhospital educational program to counteract the pervasive myths about disulfiram.

Covert sensitization, employed by Anant (1967), involves the pairing of imagined drinking behavior with imagined aversive consequences. The client is asked to think about drinking beer or liquor, and as he brings the can, bottle, or glass close to his mouth, he begins to smell the alcohol which results in a nauseous feeling followed by vomiting and dry heaving. The therapist describes in great detail the unpleasant consequences concomitant with the drinking in an attempt to provide a negative association for the client.

WHEN AND WHERE

Spouses often disagree when and where drinking alcoholic beverages is appropriate. Some spouses state that drinking is never appropriate, others that it should occur only on special occasions and at home, and still others that drinking should occur anytime and anywhere.

As in the treatment of "Who Drinks," spouses trade positive behaviors so that each gets what he wants. For example, the husband will agree to stop drinking alcohol around his in-laws in exchange for his wife making a cherry pie or chocolate cake once a week.

For other couples, the wife may want to develop a tolerance for her husband drinking alcohol anytime he chooses. In such cases, therapy would proceed as follows. Desensitization would involve pairing relaxation with the thought of the spouse drinking at specified times and places in a hierarchal arrangement. As an example, the wife may be desensitized to her husband's drinking in the presence of her parents, which, heretofore, had resulted in anxiety for her.

Selective reinforcement may involve having the drinking spouse reward the non-drinking spouse for non-nagging behavior. For instance, if the wife did not want her husband to drink at any time other than New Year's Eve, he would begin to drink small amounts of alcohol, such as one beer, at times other than the specified events, and would reinforce or reward his wife for being tolerant of his drinking behavior. Hence, Nash would tell Marilyn that he appreciated her not nagging about his drinking a Budweiser and that he would like to take her out to dinner.

Modeling may involve the client's associating with friends who approximate the desired drinking model. If Nash believes that drinking behavior is appropriate anytime, and Marilyn believes drinking appropriate only on holidays, they would be asked to socialize with couples who shared Nash's value. In this way, Marilyn could model after the other wives.

A contingency could be established by making positive, enjoyable behaviors of the wife contingent on her husband's drinking. As an example, the wife who wanted to become more tolerant of her husband's drinking would place sewing, playing bridge, using the phone, and other enjoyable activities contingent on her husband drinking at various times and places.

As can be seen, there are a number of techniques available to the therapist to assist spouses for whom alcohol is a problem. The innovative therapist will modify and extend the above techniques, as well as add other techniques to assist his clients in achieving their respective goals. In treating problems of how much alcohol, therapy should always be preceded by a consultation with the client's physician to verify the client's tolerance for alcohol and by a clear delineation of the moral and religious beliefs of both partners.

7. in-laws

Most in-law problems probably revolve around two basic issues: (1) values, and (2) problem discrimination. The value issue involves an inability or unwillingness on the part of each spouse to rank in order who they value most: relatives, parents, or the spouse. It is unusual, indeed almost impossible, for an in-law problem to develop when the spouse always chooses his partner over his parents. On the other hand, problems become colossal when spouses continually choose their respective parents over the spouse, yet say that they love the spouse more.

A second issue involves a careful discrimination of who has the problem. A wife recently decided that she would like to go on an afternoon trip with her husband (something she had not done in ten years), excluding her mother, who lived next door. When she told her mother what was planned, the mother began to cry and plead not to be left alone. The wife decided that if taking an afternoon trip with her husband displeased her mother, it was her mother who had the problem, not she. It can be seen that this wife also made a value decision by choosing her husband over her mother.

Throughout the discussion to follow, each of the above issues is involved. Marital partners must decide what their values are and decide whose problems they choose to take.

WHICH PARENTS TO VISIT

The above heading assumes that a decision has been made to visit either or both sets of parents at some time. Many couples are bored, irritated, or frustrated when visiting either set of parents, and consequently, never visit either. When the spouses are in direct conflict concerning whether one's parents should be visited, the decision is usually made for the spouse to visit his or her parents alone for a specified period of time. As an example, if Thomas does not like Theresa's parents, and they dislike him, Theresa would visit them alone for one week during the year, and during that time Thomas would go on a fishing trip, a golfing venture, or some other pleasurable activity. In this way, the stimulus value of Thomas's wife visiting her parents is positively altered.

When there is considerable discrepancy over the amount of time each feels he should spend with his parents, a compromise is made, and the Premack principle employed. If Theresa wants to spend a month with her mother and Thomas wants her to spend a week, desirable activities for each spouse would be made contingent on a compromise, such as Theresa spending two and a half weeks away.

PARENTS DISLIKE SPOUSE

There are parents who defame and degrade the spouse of their son or daughter. The son or daughter who values the spouse over the parents will tell the parents that he loves the mate and does not want to hear anything negative about his mate, and should the parents continue to speak negatively about the mate, he will discontinue seeing them. In other words, the time spent by the offspring with the parents is made contingent on the parents exuding a favorable attitude toward the spouse. Value decisions are crucial in dealing with in-law difficulties.

MEDDLING

Parents often attempt to influence the decisions of their married children. Decisions such as where to live, what kind of car to buy or home to build, how many children to have, when to have them, and what to name them are decisions in which parents (and in-laws) may try to influence their son or daughter.

There are a number of spouses who have difficulty in deciding what to do without consulting the respective parents or without being greatly influenced by their opinion. This dependence on the parents may be treated by using such techniques as systematic desensitization, selective reinforcement, modeling, covert reinforcement, stop-think, and the Premack principle.

Desensitization may be employed to reduce feelings of guilt which accompany making a decision contradictory to the parent's preference. For instance, the client referred to above felt guilty about taking a trip with her husband and leaving her mother at home. Desensitization might have been employed, hopefully producing relaxation, where previously guilt, manifested by anxiety and discomfort, had resulted from such a decision. This treatment procedure assumes that the spouse has made a decision to value her mate over her parents.

Selective reinforcement may involve having the spouse reward the partner for making decisions independent of one's parents. As an example, when Jerry made an independent decision, Linda would tell him that she was proud of him and happily married.

Modeling may be employed by identifying people in the client's social world who are weaned from their parents, and having the client talk to them about how they became independent of their parents. In addition, the counselor may also serve as a model for appropriate responses to parents where opinions between parent and offspring differ.

Covert reinforcement would involve the client thinking pleasurable and desirable thoughts following an independent decision. In other words, Linda would think about the new dress she had recently purchased immediately following a decision to place her child in a kindergarten of which her mother disapproved. Making an independent decision involves listening to all the facts and opinions, including those from one's parents, and, then, making a decision.

The stop-think technique may be useful when Linda begins to ruminate about the consequences of deciding against her parents' preference. She can say aloud to herself, "Stop" and, at that time, get out an index card on which has been written a number of competing thoughts, such as "Both Jerry and I are proud of me when I don't let my folks buffalo me."

The Premack principle may be employed by placing desirable, adaptive, pleasurable behaviors contingent on independent decision making. As an example, Jerry's fishing and golf afternoons would be contingent on making an independent decision concerning what car to buy. It cannot be overemphasized that the creative therapist will modify, extend, or develop the techniques which are useful in assisting his particular clients with their particular problems.

MONEY

Financial problems with in-laws develop when the married couple do not discriminate between borrowing and receiving, and their parents do not discriminate between lending and giving. Borrowing implies an intent to repay. A couple who borrow money from their parents do so with the intention of repaying the money at some specified time. In the same way, parents who lend money do so with the intention of being repaid. Parents who lend their son or daughter money to complete his or her education expect to be repaid.

Receiving, however, does not imply the intent to repay. A couple who receive money or goods in the form of furniture, car, etc., do so with the awareness that repayment is not required. In the same way, a gift is a gift only if it is given without the expectation of a return. A gift does not imply an exchange.

Financial in-law problems develop when parents or in-laws (or both) think they are giving when they are actually lending, and their children think they are receiving when they are actually borrowing. A coed whose parents were paying for her education said that she had to do what her parents said or they would terminate her funds. In effect, the money for her education was not a gift, but was a loan which implied the right of the parents to control the behavior of their daughter. Her repayment was in the form of acquiescing to her parents' desires.

As is true with most marital problems, discriminations must be made, and values must be chosen. In the above situation, the girl must make the discrimination between receiving and borrowing. Having decided that borrowing is the issue, she must now decide whether she chooses her independence over borrowing or vice-versa. If she chooses independence as her first value, she would not accept gifts or aid from her parents which are not, in fact, gifts. If her parents are unwilling to give instead of loan, she might decide to stop "borrowing" from them. As might be expected, she chose to borrow.

A number of clients, both husbands and wives, say that they feel obligated to engage in certain behaviors (i.e., visits) for their parents and in-laws as a result of money or aid which has been given by them. This obligation is a response to an unwillingness or inability to discriminate between receiving and borrowing. This discrimination does not imply that mutual reinforcement and exchange should not be present in child-parent relations. Rather, mutual reinforcement or exchange, is desirable for both families involved. On the other hand, it is crucial to know what issues are involved and what choices are being made. In this way, money and in-law problems are obviated.

IN-LAWS DISLIKE IN-LAWS

It is probably wisest and best for the married couple to perceive the disagreements and dislikes which one set of parents has toward the other as being the problem between the respective parents. Hence, if Larry likes Carolyn's parents, he will not become upset if his parents choose not to interact with her parents—as long as he does not take their problem. Disagreements should be left where the disagreements are—between the in-laws. Who has the problem?—the in-laws.

SPOUSE DISLIKES IN-LAWS

A husband recently seen in counseling had been accused by his mother-in-law of having an extramarital relationship. The husband indicated that the accusation had been without basis, and had resulted in a complete break with his mother-in-law. Although his house was adjacent to the property of his mother-in-law, it had been several years since they had interacted socially. However, the wife had continued to see her mother often.

It is crucial, in dealing with this type of problem, that the hierarchal values of the mate be specified. In effect, to keep in-law problems at a minimum, the spouses should always value each other over their parents and in-laws. In the above situation, it was imperative to have the wife specify her hierarchal values relative to her husband and her mother. It was only after the wife consciously chose her husband as her first value that the in-law problem began to improve.

Why was the problem not left between the spouse and the in-law? Married people often have the problems of one another. This is particularly true in in-law relationships.

Additional treatment procedures for dealing with the above problem may involve systematic desensitization and avoidance forever. Desensitization would involve reducing the anxiety of the spouse in the presence of the in-law. A hierarchy of situations would be arranged, relaxation would be induced, and mental images of specific scenes would be paired with relaxation. Desensitization (concomitant with role playing) may be employed prior to the involvement of the spouse in a social situation with the in-law which may increase the probability of adaptive functioning in that situation.

With some in-law relationships, avoidance forever is the only workable solution. This is particularly true when the motivation for an improved relationship is one-sided. Thus, if the in-law will not respond to an invitation to dinner, dessert, or a ride to the lake, the problem remains with that in-law. There are some husbands and wives who see their in-laws twice in their lifetimes, at weddings and at funerals.

8. friends

Behaviorally, friendships are defined as positive feelings of two people for each other which result from favorable interaction over time. Accordingly, the husband who spends time with his colleagues and associates will establish friendships with them, as the wife will become friends with those with whom she spends time. It often occurs that the husband does not like those with whom his wife spends her time, just as the wife may not like her husband's friends.

DIFFERENT FRIENDS

In dealing with the problem of different friends, it is crucial to keep the issues separate. It is not unusual for a spouse to say that he does not like a friend of the spouse when actually he is concerned about the amount of time his spouse is spending with that friend. Lucy may confuse the issue of her desire for more time with Fred with the issue of her dislike for one of his friends. In this case, the counselor should treat the problem of mutual time, rather than her dislike for his friend.

On the other hand, there may be a genuine dislike for one of the spouse's friends. As an alternative to continuing to dislike the spouse's friend, the decision may be made to attempt to develop a more positive attitude toward that friend. Procedures such as contingency structuring, desensitization, modeling, selective reinforcement, and incompatible responding may be used to achieve a more favorable relationship. If James did not like Sylvia's friend, a contingency might be established by making pleasurable activities for James contingent on Sylvia spending time with her friend. As an example, James's fishing trips and golf matches would be contingent on Sylvia's spending time with her friend. In this way, the stimulus event (Sylvia with friend) is assigned a more positive value and results in enjoyable activities for James.

Desensitization may be employed where James experiences considerable anxiety when thinking about Sylvia being with her friend. In addition, James may experience anxiety when he is near Sylvia's friend. In both situations, a hierarchy of anxiety-provoking events would be listed and arranged from the event which evoked the least amount of anxiety to that which evoked the greatest. Following the arrangement of the hierarchy, relaxation would be induced and mental images of the hierarchal events would be presented to James. To assist in the generalization of the desensitization procedure and to assess its effectiveness, the client may be asked to engage in a number of behaviors listed on the hierarchy.

Lazarus (1968) noted the effectiveness of rehearsal desensitization which involves the therapist and his client role playing the anxiety-producing situations arranged in a hierarchal sequence. In this situation, various encounters with Sylvia's friend would be role played by James and the therapist, with the therapist modeling the behaviors which he feels James should exhibit in the presence of Sylvia's friend. These behaviors are then enacted by James with the therapist (or female model) playing the role of Sylvia's friend. If James becomes anxious playing a particular role, an event lower on the hierarchal sequence would be enacted.

Modeling may involve not only the preceding role playing sequence, but also may entail the spouse engaging in social situations in which a friend of the same sex interacts favorably with the friend in question. As an example, if one of James's friends likes Sylvia's friend, a social event should be arranged so that James could observe his friend interacting with Sylvia's friend. In this way, James might assume a more positive attitude towards his wife's friend.

Selective reinforcement would involve Sylvia reinforcing James for positive, favorable, adaptive responses, both verbal and nonverbal, toward her friend. In essence, when James said, "Let's have your friend over for a daiquiri," Sylvia would ask, "Where would you like to go on our vacaction?" She would also tell him that she appreciates his willingness to try to get along with her friend. It should be understood that in many cases, spouses are actually reinforced for negative verbal and nonverbal behavior relative to a friend. For example, a spouse usually responds to a negative statement about a friend with resentment and frustration, but always with attention and concern, which may result in increasing that negative behavior. The spouse may be inadvertently maintaining the very behaviors which he chooses to extinguish.

Incompatible behaviors may also assist the client in achieving a more positive attitude toward the friend of the spouse. James may begin by having Sylvia relay a positive message to her friend. As an example, James would ask Sylvia to tell Jane "hello." In this way, a positive attitude may be stimulated in Jane toward James, which may make their subsequent interaction more pleasant. The basic premise of incompatible behaviors is that feelings and attitudes are based on behaviors, and that under certain conditions, these feelings and attitudes do and do not occur. Jane is more likely to feel positive about James if he behaves in a positive, adaptive way toward her. Behaviors of friendship are incompatible with attitudes of hostility. In effect, a more favorable attitude will often follow positive behaviors since an individual frequently can act himself into a new way of thinking more quickly than he can think himself into a new way of acting.

As can be seen, an incompatible response has an effect in two ways: (1) James begins to feel more positive and more tolerant toward Sylvia's friend, and (2) Jane begins to behave in more adaptive ways toward James, which results in James having more positive feelings toward her. Thus, a mutual cycle of reinforcement is established and replaces a pattern of withdrawal with subsequent loss of interpersonal reinforcement.

It should not be overlooked that in some cases one spouse may be unable to interact with friends of his partner because of differential interests and knowledge in a particular area. A wife with a Ph.D. in economics and her husband, an athletic coach with a high school education, indicated that they had difficulty relating to the spouse's friends. Their problem of different friends was improved by their agreement to maintain respective friends and to develop mutual friends who were not dependent on his job or hers. Social contacts (neighbors) were sought and established so that this core of relationships supplemented their respective friendships.

The preceding techniques may be utilized to assist a reluctant spouse to achieve a more positive attitude toward the friends of the mate. In other situations, it may be more adaptive for the spouse to spend specified periods of time with the friend independent of the time with the mate. If Sylvia's friend, Jane, enjoys a particular activity, such as ceramics, the couple may decide that Sylvia will spend one afternoon a week with Jane discussing ceramics, while James uses that time to play golf or visit one of his friends.

AMOUNT OF TIME WITH FRIENDS

Couples often disagree on how much time one spouse should spend with a friend independent of the attitude toward that friend. Elaine may not mind Pete spending an afternoon fishing with his friend, but she may become distraught when he returns at 11:00 P.M. The disagreement is one over time, and not over whether the friendship should exist. Treatment may involve having each spouse specify how much time he feels is appropriate for the partner to spend with the respective friend, identify a compromise, and establish a contingency whereby the positive behaviors of each are made contingent on that compromise. If Pete felt that six hours a week were appropriate and Elaine felt that two hours were appropriate, his fishing and her shopping would be made contingent on four hours with the friend.

NUMBER OF FRIENDS

Number of friends is a problem for some couples who complain not of too many, but of too few close, interpersonal relationships. In essence, these couples indicate that they have no friends with whom to socialize. The behavioral clinician would treat nonsocial behavior as any other behavior and would assume that it is an inappropriate, learned response to other people. Obviously, certain localities are more conducive to social interaction than others, which often provide convenient rationalizations and excuses for couples who have no friends.

Graduated responses, modeling, the Premack principle, and selective reinforcement may be useful in treating asocial behaviors of clients. Establishing friendships would involve having the counselor identify with the clients possible social partners in their community and having them initiate interaction with these couples. As an example, the husband or wife would call a couple and invite them to dinner, dessert, movie, or a sporting event. The assumption is made that friendships develop as a result of favorable activities occurring together in time. Graduated responses would be involved since at first the couple may not choose to spend an entire evening with anyone else, but would prefer to spend small segments of time so that they might get to know others while anxiety is at a low level. For some couples, an evening meal would be inappropriate since that would require too much time interacting; thus a dessert or a Sunday afternoon visit may be more appropriate initially.

Modeling may be used to assist the clients in acquiring the social skills necessary to develop social relationships. The counselor would play the role of the client meeting a new acquaintance (played by the client), after which the client would model after the counselor. Some individuals become anxious when anticipating their initial behaviors toward someone new, and can best overcome these feelings of hesitancy by modeling after another.

The Premack principle may be employed by having the couple place their respective desirable behaviors contingent on social interaction with others. One contingency might be that they only go to a movie or to the beach on the condition that another couple accompanies them.

Selective reinforcement would involve having the spouses verbally and interpersonally reinforce each other for positive approach behaviors concerning other people. As an example, Stan would tell Barbara that he thought it was very nice that she invited the neighbors to dinner. This verbal reward would be accompanied by his hugging and kissing her in an effort to display his warm feelings toward her for acting in a positive way toward others. In the same way, Barbara would notice the positive approach behaviors of Stan, and express verbal and physical approval of these behaviors.

The basic treatment plan in assisting the couple with too few friends is that of involving them with others in a systematic, positive way. A familiar adage states, "He who would have a friend must first be one." The therapist can do no less than increase the positive approach behaviors of his socially deprived clients.

CONFIDENCES TO FRIENDS

Husbands and wives often complain that the spouse continually reveals confidences to friends. In essence, they feel that the content of what they share should not be revealed to others. Often, a wife complains that her husband tells his friends about their sexual relationship. Hence, she becomes angry when she learns that her husband has told a friend that she has an intrauterine device. Likewise, a husband may become upset when his wife reveals his salary to the neighbors.

Treatment of the disagreement over confidences to friends entails an agreement between the partners concerning what specifically is to be labeled "ours" and "theirs." As an example, matters which relate to money, contraception, and childrearing difficulties may be labeled as "ours," whereas plans for a new house, the impending vacation, and the new stereo may be labeled as "theirs." What is labeled as "ours" is to be discussed only between the partners, and that labeled "theirs" may be discussed with anyone.

An exchange contract would be made whereby the husband would agree not to talk about contraception and childrearing difficulties in return for his wife agreeing not to discuss her husband's finances with others. In addition, each spouse should selectively reward his partner for fulfilling his part of the agreement. As an example, George should notice that Cindy chose not to discuss a particular issue (their finances) when they were with their neighbors even though it may have been convenient to do so. He would give her verbal and behavioral reinforcement for engaging in this type of silent behavior.

Happiness dies if it is not shared (Wright, 1970). Friendships allow married couples to increase their enjoyment in life by sharing it with others. Dr. Edgar Arendall, a minister, has as part of his marriage ceremony the phrase, "And they shall double each other's joys and halve the sorrows." This too can be said of friendships.

9. religion

The concept of religion represents a system of values which reflects a standard of behavior after which one may pattern his life. In counseling a couple whose problems center around religion, it is crucial, at the outset, for the respective partners to decide, in a hierarchal arrangement, their values relative to religion and the spouse. Since each religion demands of its followers that they engage in specified behaviors, the husband or wife must decide whether or not the spouse takes precedence over the religious values. If the wife decides that she chooses her religion over her husband, the husband may value living without his wife, rather than living with a wife who values her religion more than him. Time in therapy will be useless until these value decisions and discriminations are made.

DIFFERENT RELIGIONS

Protestant-Catholic, Catholic-Jewish, and Protestant-Jewish marriages result in two respective, and often distinct, value systems joined together. In addition, various combinations of agnosticism, atheism, and theism result in behavioral problems in marriage.

Therapy proceeds by identifying the alternatives available to a couple: (1) worship independently, (2) one spouse adopt the religion of the other, (3) both spouses identify a compromising religion and adopt its value system. Behavioral techniques are used to assist the client in reaching the goal of his choice. As an example, if the couple have chosen to worship independently, a number of therapeutic rules will be established: (1) a contingency may be established by making the pleasurable behaviors for one mate contingent on the worship of the partner. As an example, Bill's flying lesson becomes contingent on Sue's attendance at Mass. (2) The non-worshiping mate is to ask honest questions concerning what occurred in the church service, and (3) the worshiping mate is to selectively reinforce his mate's positive questioning, both verbally and nonverbally. As an example, when Sue returns from Mass, Bill is to ask her how the service was, to which she is to reply that she enjoyed it and hopes that it is a pleasant day for flying. As can be seen, arguments do not develop in situations so structured that the behaviors of one partner result in pleasurable behaviors for the other.

Should the couple decide that their goal is for one of them to adopt the religious dogma of the other, the therapist assists in modifying the attitude of the spouse toward that particular religion. The assumption is made that a positive attitude will result from specific behaviors occurring in time and that a new attitude will not develop out of nowhere. For that reason, the therapist structures specific activities and behaviors in which the client is expected to engage in order to develop a more favorable attitude. As an example, assuming that Bill is desirous of becoming more tolerant of the Catholic faith, he would be expected to attend Mass with Sue once each month at a time of his own choosing and to make fishing (a pleasurable activity) contingent on his attendance. In addition, the couple would be instructed to invite Catholic neighbors to their home for a social event (not a church event). Also, for each friendship which Bill develops with a member of the church, the couple may decide to allocate a certain amount of money to be utilized to buy something which Bill values, such as a fishing boat.

Having been to church on a number of occasions and established several relationships with members in the church, Bill would then ask to become a part of a particular church activity, such as taking up the offering, chairing a church committee, etc. It is this type of involvement in the church which will result in interpersonal reward for Bill and which may assist in a more positive attitude toward Sue's religion. One may wonder if such a silly program actually results in a changed attitude. The program rests on the assumption that the spouse has made a value decision to improve the relationship with his wife, which included a changed attitude toward religion. The situation so structured involves reinforcement from his wife, friends within the church, and subsequently, self-reinforcement. Such reinforcement should help the spouse maintain a positive attitude over time.

Should the couple decide to compromise their respective religions and seek an alternative, each of the above suggestions for increasing one's tolerance for a particular religion may be utilized. The couple would place desirable, positive behaviors contingent on church attendance, would instigate friendships among church members, and would participate in the functioning of the church itself. A decision to develop a positive attitude toward a third religion or church requires specific behaviors designed to achieve that end.

RITUALS

Some decisions must be made in which there are no gray areas. As an example, a couple may disagree over their respective wishes concerning a religious ritual. Bill may want Sue to use the pill, whereas, Sue may refuse to use any type of contraception since doing so would conflict with her religious values. The therapist would respond to this situation by having the partners respectively indicate on a 10-point continuum their desires for birth control by any means. Should Bill say that he desired birth control at a level of 10, and Sue indicate that she desired birth control at a level of zero, the therapist would ask that they rank their values relative to religion and the mate. Were Bill to rank his desire not to have a baby over his desire to stay married to Sue, and if Sue were to rank her religion over Bill, the couple would have two alternatives: (1) maintain the relationship with continued sexual frustration, or (2) terminate the marriage.

Had Bill indicated that he valued their marriage at a level of 7 and had Sue valued their relationship at a level of 9, therapy would be oriented toward increasing Sue's tolerance for the pill or some other means of contraception acceptable to her. Four techniques, alone or in combination, may be used to increase her tolerance: (1) consequences identified, (2) Premack principle, (3) selective reinforcement, and (4) covert reinforcement. The consequences of bearing a child against the expressed wishes of the husband would be explored by having Sue write an essay detailing and listing the negative consequences of having a child at this time, as well as the positive results of delaying conception. Cognitive dissonance is the goal of this exercise.

The Premack principle may be employed by having the wife engage in favorable, pleasurable activities contingent on the use of some type of contraception. As an example, if Sue particularly enjoyed talking on the phone, doing so would be contingent on taking the pill or inserting the diaphragm. In addition, she may earn the privilege of worship by using some form of contraception. As an example, seven pills punched out would be the ticket for Mass on Sunday. Therefore, the use of contraception would no longer be a stimulus for guilt, but rather a stimulus for worship and other pleasurable behaviors.

Selective reinforcement may be used by having the husband verbally approve of his wife's engaging in contraceptive behavior, as well as behaviorally reinforcing her (surprise gifts) contingent on the maintenance of this behavior over time. It should be understood that it is possible that the husband may have been rewarding his wife for not using contraception by his attention and exhortations.

Covert reinforcement may be employed by the wife directly in that she would present herself with a favorable mental image subsequent to contraceptive behavior, i.e., taking the pill, inserting the diaphragm, or inserting foam. In addition, she might present the cognition that delaying children at this time means a better world for her children in the future since her husband would be receptive at a later time, and the income would be greater to accommodate the financial needs of the child.

CHILDREN

Which religion children are encouraged to adopt is a value decision of the parents. It is they who decide what ethical cognitive constructs their children develop. It is a truism that children learn what they are taught. The problem occurs when parents disagree over what children are to be taught. This is a value decision which the parents must make, with the therapist's role being that of assisting them in considering the alternatives and in looking constructively at the consequences.

As has been said, therapy cannot proceed without the partners first making a commitment to each other in terms of ranking their values for each other over other values. As an example, if Sue values her religion over her husband when the two come into conflict, Sue would choose her religion to the detriment of her marriage. It is the counselor's role to assist Sue in making her aware that she has made a choice based on her value system, and the consequences which follow are hers. Couples who choose other values over the mate are often wiser in terminating the marriage.

The alternatives available to a couple who have decided to reduce or eliminate their problems concerning the religion in which the child should be reared are as follows: (1) teach the child both religions, (2) teach the child the religion of the more devout parent, and (3) disregard teaching the child anything. The first alternative involves teaching the child that there is no one or best religion and that there are happy, kind, devout, and honest people in all religions. In the same way, the child will be taught that his parents happen to have different beliefs about religion, but nevertheless, are very much in love with each other and are very happy. It follows that since each believes his own religion, each would take the child to his respective church and attempt to expose or influence the child to his own value system. In effect, the child may be told that he, unlike other children, will have a choice as to which religion he chooses to follow.

In reality, the child would be taken with each parent to their respective places of worship, and would be involved in the religious atmosphere with equal time being given to both parents. Hence, alternating Saturdays or Sundays would involve the child being taken to the respective houses of worship. In the event that one parent adopts atheism or agnosticism as his value system or religion, the parent would be encouraged to spend an amount of time equal to that which the other parent spends with the child explaining his beliefs and why. It is assumed that the parent who is unwilling to take the time to discuss religious and ethical values with his child does not, in fact, value such, and hence, is unconcerned about his child having his particular value structure.

A second alternative would involve having the child reared in the faith of the more devout. Devoutness would be ascertained by having each spouse independently indicate on a 10-point continuum his degree of devoutness for a particular value system or religion, with the more devout parent being given charge of the religious teaching of the child. In the event that the parents are equally devout, the first alternative may be more feasible. However, in most disagreements relative to the religion of the children, one parent emerges as being the more devout.

As can be seen, the second alternative does not involve the confusion which may occur should the child be exposed to two religions at the same time and intensity. Being reared in the faith of the more devout parent, the child not only has a good model, but may become more firmly grounded in one specific value system. From a sociological viewpoint, it is more valuable to the child that he be exposed to one specific value sytem. In this way, having established a standard, he can more accurately evaluate the alternatives available to him. In essence, confusion along idealistic lines results when no particular standard is present, and stability of values results when a core of values is identified and believed.

To assist the parent or the less devout spouse in having a positive attitude about having his or her child being reared in that faith, a contingency may be utilized by making pleasurable behaviors for that parent contingent on the church attendance or religious indoctrination of the child.

Teaching the child no religion is, in effect, teaching him a religion. Couples who allow the child to choose for himself are teaching the child that no value system is a value system and is an alternative to other value systems.

To repeat, the problem of which religion the child should be reared in is a value decision which the parents must make, with the therapist's role being that of presenting the alternatives and consequences for the various decisions. In effect, the values of the therapist will be involved in that his discussion of the alternatives and consequences would imply a particular choice on his part. The writer believes that the best alternative is rearing the child in the faith of the more devout since the advantages of this alternative include a solid identification with one value system, and the elimination of confusion at an age when standards are not present.

TITHING

Tithing is a value in many Western religions. It may also be a value to those who make and who spend money. It is not unusual for a couple to disagree concerning the ethics of tithing which are reflective of their particular religious values. This disagreement usually manifests itself in the form of the husband or wife wanting to put the tithing money into some other source. As an example, Bill would like to put the money which he and Sue earn into a fund with which to buy a car. On the other hand, Sue may feel that it is appropriate that this money should be given as the tithe and may reject Bill's request to establish a car fund with the tithing money.

A workable solution results in the spouse tithing the money which becomes available to that spouse. As an example, Sue may tithe her clothing and spending money. In effect, she is tithing a portion of that which she has received. Another alternative is for Sue, who values tithing, to get a job to pay not only the tithe for her husband's income, but also for her own income. Those who particularly value tithing and refer to it as a problem in marriage may choose the second alternative. Hence, the spouse who believes that tithing is a value will procure the money necessary to pay the tithe.

It should be clear that couples who argue over religion are arguing over values, and that those who truly have values dispense with the need for argumentation. Hence, if either Sue or Bill values religion in the form of church attendance, no birth control, indoctrination of children; or tithing, over the mate, they will always choose the religious value, which will often result in the termination of the marriage. In essence, the "true Christian" will sacrifice one's spouse for one's God. An engaged couple, one Catholic, one Protestant, were seen recently in counseling. They were concerned about whether they should get married. Since it was made clear that a hierarchy of values must be established, the girl chose her boy friend over her religion and he chose her over his religion. Hence, when their values were arranged in a systematic way, both became aware that they would not allow their religions to interfere with the marriage. They married. Such value decisions are crucial in life and in marriage counseling.

10. money

The literature in the area of marriage and the family indicates that money is one of the most frequent problems encountered in marriage. Blood (1969) has detailed the symbolic notions of money relative to control, security, etc., and has indicated that money is a very powerful force in marriage. The focus of the behavioral counselor as he treats money problems in marriages will be primarily on the behaviors which occur on the part of the spouses in regard to obtaining and managing money rather than its subjective or symbolic meaning.

AMOUNT OF MONEY

A young, pregnant wife recently sobbed in a tearful tone, "My husband simply does not make enough money for us." She began to detail the experience of living in a small, unventilated home. The tearful wife, bewildered in her third pregnancy, said that her husband did not make enough money to provide the necessary food, clothing, and shelter for the family. She noted that while her neighbors had air conditioners, washing machines, and dishwashers, they had old fans and a big wash tub. The husband, whose salary was $5,000, said that he thought his salary was low, but not inadequate and that his wife merely wanted him for the material goods which he could provide.

Two behaviors, withdrawal of financial reinforcement by the husband and withdrawal of intercourse by the wife, were being mutually maintained, one by the other. The wife noted that she was refusing to have intercourse with her husband because she felt that he was a poor provider and that he did not care enough to give her and the children the material necessities of life. The husband, on the other hand, said that he withheld his resources because he did not want to support a woman who would not have intercourse with him. A self-perpetuating, mutually negative response cycle had been established. Treatment for a couple who have an insufficient income may involve one or more of several alternatives: (1) moonlighting, (2) involving spouse in the work force, (3) using assets, (4) reducing expenditures, and (5) self-producing. Moonlighting may be effective in reducing temporary debts, i.e., birth of a child, a car accident, a new car, and may be functional if not prolonged. However, there is a point at which moonlighting loses its financial value and begins to cost the couple in terms of their positive interpersonal relationship. Moonlighting should be considered as a useful and functional, but temporary, alternative.

Involving the spouse in the work force results in an immediate increase in income. In addition, part-time or full time employment of the wife not only reduces family debts, but will concomitantly result in an immediate reduction in the anxiety of the couple since something is being done to increase the income.

Most families have some assets. The couple referred to above had several hundred sheep, some of which could be sold to supplement the existing income. Other families may have assets in the form of savings accounts or furniture and goods which can be converted into cash. The counselor should explore with the couple the availability of assets upon which they might draw for temporary financial assistance.

Reducing expenditures implies that the family would identify precisely how the money is being spent and eliminate all expenditures which are not mutually defined as necessary. These unnecessary expenditures may be in the form of color TV, air conditioning, or a second car.

Self-production is probably one of the most useful and productive means of alleviating some expenditures. As an example, a spring or summer garden may produce fresh vegetables, raising chickens results in eggs and poultry, while sewing reduces the cost of clothes and drapes. A latent function of self-production is an increase in the amount of interpersonal activity. Couples who share in the creation of a garden and its resultant harvest often increase the intensity of positive feelings for each other.

An increase in the amount of income or a decrease in the expenditures is not an easy accomplishment for some couples. However, it is only by the systematic identification of necessary expenditures and a mutual decision concerning each spouse's contribution to the alleviation of the financial problem that an improved financial position will result.

SOURCE OF MONEY

A husband and wife often disagree how money should be acquired for family use. A wife recently indicated that she felt extremely uncomfortable spending the money her husband had acquired through gambling. Another wife said that she did not like her husband getting money from his father, whereas another said that speculating in the stock market was very foolish. Gambling, borrowing money from parents or in-laws, or playing the stock market are income sources over which couples may disagree.

The source of income is a value issue. Some husbands value gambling, speculating or investing in the stock market, or borrowing from parents or in-laws, whereas some wives label these behaviors as "stupid," "inappropriate," or "inexcusable." Where disagreement exists over gambling, spouses should indicate on 10-point continuums their values in regard to gambling and their marriage (see Figures 2 and 3).

IMPORTANCE OF GAMBLING

HUSBAND

1 2 3 4 5 6 7 <u>8 9 10</u>

WIFE

<u>1 2 3</u> 4 5 6 7 8 9 10

FIGURE 2

Husband values gambling between 8 and 10. Wife values gambling between 1 and 3.

IMPORTANCE OF MAINTAINING THE MARRIAGE

HUSBAND

1 2 3 4 <u>5 6</u> 7 8 9 10

WIFE

1 2 3 4 5 6 7 8 <u>9 10</u>

FIGURE 3

Husband values marriage between 5 and 6. Wife values marriage between 9 and 10.

As can be seen, the wife values her marriage more than her dislike for gambling when the two are in conflict. Contingency structuring, selective reinforcement, extinction, covert reinforcement, desensitization, incompatible responding, and modeling may be used to assist Kathleeen in developing a more positive attitude toward Jim's gambling.

Contingency structuring may involve making the pleasurable, positive behaviors of Kathleen contingent on the gambling behavior of her husband. The rule would be made that she could write letters to close friends, use the phone, or sew only on Jim's nights out for gambling. In addition, assuming Jim had a regular job, Kathleen would buy clothes only with the money that Jim won as a result of gambling. In this way, Jim's gambling assumes a new and more positive stimulus value for Kathleen.

Selective reinforcement would involve having Jim reinforce Kathleen, verbally and nonverbally, for non-nagging behavior relative to his gambling. As an example, when Jim returns from his evening card game, he would tell Kathleen that it is nice to come home to a pleasant wife. In addition he would spend time with her that evening and talk with her about the things which happened that day in her life or their plans for a summer vacation.

Extinction would involve ignoring inappropriate, negative verbalizations. Jim would not respond to criticism concerning his gambling, but would withdraw, bodily, from the house if his wife continued.

Desensitization may be used by having Kathleen draw up a list of situations which were anxiety-provoking for her, training her to relax, and systematically presenting to her the items on her hierarchy. The successful result of desensitization would be that Kathleen could think about Jim's sitting at a card table, gambling with their savings, without a response of anxiety.

Covert reinforcement may involve Kathleen's thinking of a particular pleasant event which is to occur, e.g., husband's returning or a vacation, following such thoughts as "Jim derives a great deal of pleasure out of gambling," or "Jim and I are happier when we are not talking about his gambling."

Modeling may be used by having the spouse interact with wives who have a favorable attitude toward their husbands' gambling. In this way, she would be exposed to a number of situations in which she could observe her friends responding in a positive, adaptive way toward their husbands' gambling.

The judicious use of each of the preceding techniques is dependent on the identification of the respective value systems of the mates. It is the therapist's responsibility to help his clients achieve their goals. In the case just cited, Jim valued gambling more than he valued Kathleen, whereas Kathleen valued her husband more than her dislike for gambling. Therefore increasing Kathleen's tolerance for Jim's gambling was dependent on her decision to maintain their marriage.

Of course, the counselor should first attempt to resolve the disagreement by assisting the couple in reaching a compromise and establishing a contractual agreement. For example, the husband would agree to reduce his gambling to a specified amount ($25.00 per week) in return for his wife engaging in a behavior he enjoyed—approaching him for intercourse twice each week. However, some spouses are unwilling to compromise.

WORKING WIFE

King, McIntyre, and Axelson (1968) noted that investigations of the relationship between employment of the wife and marital satisfaction or adjustment have been inconclusive. Whereas Burgess and Cottrell (1939) found good marital adjustment was positively associated with the wife's employment, Locke and Mackprange (1949) and Applebaum (1952) noted that employment of the wife was not a significant factor in marital success. In further contrast, Axelson (1963) found that husbands of working wives showed a lower marital adjustment than husbands of non-working wives.

A working wife becomes a problem for a couple only if they define it as such. In marriages in which the husband values a wife in the traditional homemaker's role, and the wife sees her role as being the same, a marital problem relative to the working wife does not exist. On the other hand, when the wife sees her role as one of being a career woman half the time and a traditional homemaker the other half, and the husband sees his wife's role as a full time traditional homemaker, disagreements, frustrations, and conflicts result. In the same way, a husband may want a working wife, while the wife may choose to be a traditional homemaker. Thus, in all situations where value expectations differ concerning the working wife, problems will occur.

Treatment involves the spouses establishing a contractual agreement whereby each gives a behavior to get a behavior. For example, the husband who wants his wife to be a traditional homemaker agrees not to talk about his wife's employment in return for her fishing with him on Saturdays. In addition, treatment may involve increasing the husband's tolerance for his wife's employment. Specific techniques employed to increase Roger's tolerance for Maria's working may include: (1) extinction, (2) desensitization, (3) selective reinforcement, (4) modeling, and (5) contingency structuring.

Extinction may be used by having Maria bodily withdraw from any negative discussion relative to her involvement in the work force. Hence, if Roger began to complain about her working, Maria would withdraw from Roger in an effort to extinguish his verbalizations. It is understood that a value decision to become more tolerant toward Maria's working has already been established. In this way, Maria's withdrawal does not imply rejection, but implies a commitment to the value decision which each has already made. The effect of Maria's withdrawal from the discussion concerning her career hopefully would be to reduce the probability that these discussions would recur since her attention may, in fact, be maintaining her husband's negative verbalizations.

Desensitization may be employed by having the husband list on a continuum those items which resulted in anxiety for him. The lowest item might involve Maria's thinking about getting a job two months in advance, whereas the highest item might be her being an hour late coming home from work. Having listed the items in a hierarchal arrangement and having been trained to relax, Roger would be presented mental images by the therapist, beginning with the lowest item on the hierarchy. To reaffirm, the assumption of desensitization is that anxiety cannot exist with relaxation since the two behaviors are incompatible. Successful desensitization would result in Roger's ability to respond in a relaxed and comfortable way concerning his wife's employment.

Selective reinforcement would involve Maria verbally and nonverbally reinforcing Roger for positive statements about her working. As an example, when Roger asks Maria how her day was at the office, she might tell him that she would like to prepare his favorite meal and ask him what kind of dessert he would like with it, or tell him that she would like to buy him a new golf club and ask what brand he wants. In effect, any behaviors which Roger exhibited which were expressive of his positive attitude toward his wife's employment would be reinforced, initially on a continuous and later on a variable schedule.

Modeling may occur by having the husband and wife interact with couples who are happy and for whom the working wife problem is not an issue. In other words, Roger would be encouraged to observe his male friends who have working wives and to discuss with them their positive feelings concerning their wives' employment. His friends and associates would provide for him a positive model in terms of their approval of their wives being involved in the labor force.

A contingency may be established by having Roger make pleasurable activities for him contingent on Maria's involvement in the work force. As an example, Roger could only go fishing following Maria's working for one week. In this way, a previously negative event (working wife) is associated with a more pleasurable outcome (fishing trip).

As can be seen, each of the above techniques is designed to assist the husband in achieving a more positive attitude toward his wife's employment. In the case of the wife who wanted to be a career wife at a level of 5 and was married to a man who wanted her to be a traditional wife at a level of 10, treatment would be oriented toward increasing her tolerance for the traditional role. In effect, the techniques of extinction, desensitization, selective reinforcement, modeling, and contingency contracting may be used to improve her self-concept as a traditional wife. To repeat, behavioral techniques are useful only after value decisions have been made by the spouses. Until such decisions are made, therapy is not therapy, but "chit-chat" time.

SPENDING

Three value decisions must be made by each partner prior to behavioral treatment for the problem of spending. Spouses must decide their values concerning: (1) who spends, (2) how much, and (3) on what. Who spends may be directly related to how much and on what, because what is purchased at what price may depend on who is buying. As an example, in some cases the husband may decide how all money is spent, so that he decides the other issues of how much and what. Hence, who spends is more related to who decides who spends than to the person actually doing the purchasing. For example, a husband decides what specific foods are to be bought weekly and how much is to be spent on each item. In addition, he decides how much money is to be allocated for his clothes and those of his wife, and what specific clothing items are to be purchased and when. One may wonder why his wife tolerates these conditions. In effect, she has decided that her husband and marriage are of greater value than her deciding how much is spent on what.

Other couples have decided that the spouses will decide how much is spent on what in respective areas. For example, the wife will decide what foods are bought at what prices, whereas the husband will decide what materials at what prices are to be purchased for the construction of their home. Such an arrangement of respective responsibility for spending is functional to the degree that each partner is given full responsibility for his respective area. As an example, if Jane is given complete domain of the purchase of food, she could ask Barry for suggestions concerning the menu, but she should make the final decision of what is bought and at what price. In the same way, Barry may choose to consult Jane concerning what materials to purchase for the home, but the final decision would be his. Hence, an agreement to spend respectively is an agreement only if the responsibility in that area is complete, and not contingent on the approval of the other. Many spending arguments occur when the husband has given his wife money to buy something she wanted with the expectation that she spend only a portion of the cash, and later he discovered that all had been spent. In effect, the decision of who spends how much on what had not been clarified.

In dealing with the problem of who spends how much on what, the therapist would insist that his clients specify their values relative to each of these issues. Accordingly, the therapist would insist that the clients state their values concerning: who spends—the husband or wife or both; how much—to be established by each independently or by a mutual budget; and on what—a decision made by the husband or wife or both. Where disagreements exist concerning these issues, e.g., the husband feels that he should buy everything and the wife feels that she should have some spending power, a compromise is reached and exchange contracts established. In addition, the more tolerant spouse is assisted in increasing that tolerance.

Who spends is often directly related to how much is spent and what is purchased. If necessary, the husband or wife would discuss in detail their ideas concerning each of these issues. As an example, Jane may believe that money should be spent for furniture or for a bicycle for the child and indicate what she believes to be a reasonable amount for each. In addition, she may believe that a new washing machine is necessary and state the amount she feels should be spent. In the same way, Barry would state what purchases he would choose to make, such as an outboard motor or a new stereo system, and indicate what amount he would choose to spend for each.

Problems occur when spouses differ over the object to be purchased and the amount to be spent. As an example, the purchase of a stereo may obviate the purchase of furniture. The therapist would deal with this situation by identifying the respective values of the couple concerning who has been given responsibility for the final decision when the two come into conflict. In the preceding example, both alternatives may be impossible to accomplish simultaneously. However, if the couple have previously decided who will make the final decision when a conflict occurs, spending problems are alleviated. Therefore, should Barry decide to buy the stereo, it would be assumed that this was his value for their marriage and would imply that the next expenditure may go toward furniture or something that Jane wanted. If, in fact, Barry always chose to spend money to the exclusion of Jane's wishes, Jane would have the decision of tolerating this lower status on Barry's hierarchy of values or terminating the relationship. Hence, marital couples who have as their first value their marriage will not consistently choose values which deviate markedly from those of their mate.

A husband recently indicated that his wife was incapable of making sensible decisions relative to the purchase of furniture. He noted that she was careless in her purchases and would often buy furniture at an unreasonable price when it could be bought elsewhere cheaper. In addition, he noted that she was not careful in the selection of furniture since she would inevitably purchase furniture which was imperfect. Therapy consisted of allocating to the wife a specified amount of money monthly which she could spend on whatever she chose without approval of her husband. This resulted in careful selection on her part and in a reconstruction of the belief on the part of the husband that she could select and purchase sensibly.

Money problems are probably the most difficult for the behavior therapist to treat since doing so is often dependent on the reconstruction of values and cognitions which have existed for years. However, the treatment of spending problems should proceed with the behavioristic assumption—behavior is learned.

Having identified on a 10-point continuum the more tolerant spouse with reference to the issues—who spends, how much, on what—a goal of therapy would be to increase the tolerance of that spouse. Desensitization, extinction, selective reinforcement, modeling, and contingency structuring may be utilized to achieve this end.

Assuming that Jane wanted to have money available to her for independent spending at a level of 10, and Barry wanted her not to do so at a level of 5, Barry would be asked to construct a hierarchy of items ranging from the least to the greatest anxiety, would be trained to relax, and while relaxed, would be presented by the therapist the items on the hierarchy, beginning with the lowest item. As an example, when deep muscle relaxation had been induced, the therapist would ask Barry to think about Jane in a downtown store about to purchase a handkerchief for him. When Barry could think about this scene after three presentations without an increase in anxiety, the therapist would move to the next item, which may be Jane purchasing perfume for herself.

Extinction would involve termination of the arguments (loud verbalizations) concerned with spending by having Jane or Barry bodily withdraw from the situation. When Barry became loud when talking about Jane's spending, she would withdraw from the room and, thus, terminate the negative interaction.

Likewise, selective reinforcement may be employed by having Jane, both verbally and behaviorally, reinforce Barry for neutral or positive statements concerning her spending. If Barry were to say, "This handkerchief shows fine craftsmanship" or "I like that perfume," Jane would tell him, "Thank you," accompanied by a kiss, and ask him which favorite meal he would like that evening.

Modeling may be employed by having Barry discuss with his male friends who had wives who spent judiciously, the merits of having a wife who makes independent decisions concerning purchasing at some predefined level. For instance, Jane may not choose to decide what furniture is bought for the house without discussion with her husband, whereas she might choose to buy this week's groceries or a new bedspread on her own.

Contingency structuring may be employed by making the desirable, positive activities for Barry contingent on Jane's spending. In effect, his golfing, fishing, and flying would be contingent on her having made three independent purchasing decisions that same week.

To reiterate, spending decisions are value decisions with the above techniques being utilized only after the identification and specification of values concerning who spends how much on what. Indeed, some husbands and wives will choose not to live with each other when these values are specified, whereas others may be willing to achieve a meaningful compromise.

BOOKKEEPING

Bookkeeping refers to who is responsible for managing the income of the family. It is usually best for one spouse to be responsible for an up-to-date checkbook, particularly when a joint account, rather than separate accounts, exists. Usually, married couples who divide the responsibility of bookkeeping do not make the specific, respective responsibilities clear, with resultant confusion, frustration, and an overdrawn account.

Treatment of a disagreement concerning who should be the bookkeeper of family finances may involve: (1) having the partner more experienced in accounting procedures be responsible for all money matters, or (2) dividing the role responsibilities with no overlap in function. Separate checking accounts would be established with an appropriate amount of income distributed to each account. Each partner would be responsible for financial concerns in his allocated area. The husband might be responsible for house, car, and insurance payments as well as having money available for recreation, whereas his wife might be responsible for all monies pertaining to food and clothes. An agreement would be made for each partner not to take the problem of his spouse should the other be delinquent in his financial responsibilities.

The therapist is responsible for helping his clients accomplish their goals. Money problems usually require a systematic identification of the values of the spouses concerning the procuring, managing, and spending the available money. However, the identification of the goals sought represents only the beginning which must be followed by direct therapeutic intervention.

11. recreation

The American Dream insists that leisure time be available to provide fun for the plodding people of the labor force. The existence of week-ends, Labor Day, and other governmental holidays testifies to the importance of recreation in the national eye. Some individuals drag through the week only because of the impending week-end and never miss a Saturday at the lake.

Recreation becomes a problem in marriage because it represents a value choice concerning how one chooses to spend his time. It is said that life is nothing more than activities which occur in time (Madsen and Madsen, 1970). If a spouse chooses to spend his time during recreative hours alone, not only will the partner feel disgruntled, but the marriage will often deteriorate. It is assumed that meaningful relationships are dependent on the existence of the partners engaging in some mutually enjoyable activities. In those situations in which the partners do not spend time together, a major portion of which may be recreation, their relationship suffers. This is not to imply that couples cannot spend some of their recreative hours independent of each other and yet maintain a good relationship. However, to the extent that partners continually choose to spend their time apart, the attitudes and feelings of closeness diminish.

TYPE OF RECREATION

It is not unusual that spouses disagree over what recreational activities are appropriate. This complaint may be expressed by the wife who complains that her husband's flying is dangerous, his fishing expensive, and his duck hunting foolish. In the same way, the husband may complain about his wife's sewing, attending garden and book clubs, and playing bridge.

Treatment of a conflict in recreational interests would involve and attempt to ascertain from each spouse what behaviors he would like from his partner. For example, the wife may want her husband to limit his fishing to one twelve-hour period on Saturday, whereas the husband may want his wife to cook the fish he catches. Hence, the husband would trade being with his wife every day except Saturday for his wife cooking the fish he caught on Saturday.

Should the wife still have negative feelings about her husband's fishing, the techniques of desensitization, modeling, selective reinforcement and the Premack principle may be used to assist her in developing a more positive attitude.

Desensitization would involve the wife drawing up a list of items ranging from those of least to greatest anxiety relative to her husband's fishing, training in relaxation, and pairing of the two. Successful desensitization would result in her ability to think about her husband still fishing two hours past suppertime without anxiety.

Modeling may be employed by having the wife identify among her friends, wives who have positive, favorable attitudes toward their husbands' fishing. She would be instructed to spend one half hour each week talking with her friends about their husbands' fishing. In this way, the wife would be exposed to favorable models for tolerating fishing behavior on the part of her husband.

Selective reinforcement would involve having the husband reward his wife verbally and behaviorally for non-nagging behavior concerning his fishing. As an example, when Ingrid did not respond negatively to Bob's statement that he was going fishing, he might kiss her and tell her that he would like to take her to the country club Saturday evening. It would be just as important for Bob to ignore the nagging behavior of his wife in an attempt to extinguish it.

The Premack principle may be employed by making the enjoyable activities for Ingrid, such as sewing, shopping, and using the phone, contingent on positive statements to Bob about his fishing. In this way, she could earn one day's phone privileges by saying to Bob, "I hope it is going to be a good day for fishing." In addition, a contingency may be established whereby Ingrid would earn time in her activities contingent on Bob's fishing. Hence, his day at the lake would earn an equal amount of shopping time for her. It is understood that Ingrid could only shop and use the phone contingent on Bob's fishing behavior.

As can be seen, the above program is designed to produce a more favorable attitude in the wife toward her husband's fishing. When the wife nags her husband about his fishing and he, in turn, becomes involved in an argument with her, her negative attitude about fishing is likely to be maintained. Until systematic reinforcement for incompatible behavior occurs and until such procedures as desensitization, modeling, and the Premack principle are employed, disagreements over type of recreation will probably continue.

TIME SPENT IN RECREATION

In treating a problem concerning the type of recreation, the counselor should be alert to detect the reason for such violent opposition on the part of one spouse for the recreational activities of the partner. Not infrequently, the wife will be more concerned about how much time her husband spends in the activity, rather than the activity itself. Ingrid may not care whether her husband fishes, but does prefer that he not fish every week-end. Hence, the counselor should separate the time issue from the activity issue.

Treatment of time spent in recreation normally involves having each spouse state how much time he feels is appropriate. As an example, the husband may feel that twelve flying hours per week is not excessive, whereas his wife might indicate that six hours is more moderate. If the spouses are mutually concerned about improving their relationship, a compromise would be ascertained and a systematic setting of contingencies, coupled with selective reinforcement, would be utilized.

Since Tom and Wilma indicated respectively that twelve and six hours would be appropriate for his flying, pleasurable behaviors for each would be made contingent on a compromise of nine hours of flying per week. For example, Tom could fly nine hours one week only if he logged no more than nine hours the previous week. Should he exceed nine hours by one minute, he would forfeit one week's flying privileges. In the same way, Wilma would earn shopping and sewing behaviors contingent on her husband's logging nine hours in flight per week. If he did not log nine hours of flying time, she was not to engage in shopping or sewing.

Selective reinforcement may be used by both spouses. Tom would verbally and behaviorally reinforce Wilma for positive verbalizations about his nine hours of flying and her willingness to accede to his requests for more time in the sky. Similarly, Wilma would verbally and behaviorally reinforce Tom for confining his flying time to nine hours and his willingness to reduce the amount of time he spent near the clouds.

In conjunction with the preceding problems, specific time is always allocated for the spouses to spend in on-task interaction with each other and in specific recreational activities together. One of the divisive forces in any marriage is that the spouses spend too much time apart from each other, whereas an adhesive behavior of concerned spouses is that of spending time together.

VACATION

Spouses frequently disagree over where they would like to spend their vacations. Not infrequently, the husband would like to fish, golf, or plant a garden during his vacation, whereas his wife would like for them to visit relatives, surf at the beach, or drive through the New England States.

Behavioral treatment may involve one of three alternatives: (1) compromise, (2) increase the positive attitude of one spouse toward the vacation choice of the mate, or (3) separate vacations. In those marriages in which recreational interests overlap, a compromise of vacation choices is made. Where Carl likes fishing and Patsy likes surfing at the beach, an agreement would be made to go to the beach with specified amounts of time being allocated to Carl for fishing. In addition, time for Carl and Patsy to spend together would be specified and contingencies established to maintain that behavior. For Carl, fishing could occur only after spending one hour with Patsy on the beach.

To assist Patsy in achieving a more positive attitude toward her husband's fishing, surfing would be contingent on Carl's fishing in the afternoons. In this way, fishing, surfing, and togetherness behaviors may occur and result in positive feelings for the respective spouses.

Other compromises may occur at Christmas in which spouses agree to spend a specific amount of time with each set of in-laws or time spent with one in-law earns time for the spouse in an activity enjoyable for him. Hence, the husband could earn time hunting quail by spending time with his wife's parents.

In those cases in which compromise is not a feasible alternative, it is frequently helpful to treat the spouse more interested in maintaining the marriage in an effort to achieve a more positive attitude toward the vacation choice. When spouses are requested to indicate on 10-point continuums their values in regard to spending their vacation at a particular place and to their marriage, the husband may value the Blue Ridge Mountains at a level of 10 and his marriage at a level of 5, whereas his wife may value the beach at a level of 7, but her marriage at a level of 9. In this situation, the more motivated spouse, the wife, would be assisted in therapy toward achieving a more adaptive attitude toward spending their vacation in the mountains. The treatment program may include programming time together, desensitization, stop-think, selective reinforcement, extinction, modeling, and the Premack principle.

Programming time together would involve allocating a specified amount of time which the partners would spend together independent of where they were. As an example, if the couple had driven to Tennessee so the husband could fish in the bubbling trout streams, a specified amount of time, such as an hour daily, would be allocated for the couple to spend together. In this way, although the husband may fish much of the day, the couple would spend their evenings together in on-task interaction. It is interesting that a spouse does not complain about where the mate is as long as he knows that the mate is going to devote time to him. Nellie is not disgruntled at John's fishing during the day if she knows that he will be with her at night.

Desensitization may be employed to assist the spouse in reducing the anxiety associated with a particular vacation choice. For a wife who is afraid to visit Mammoth Cave because of her claustrophobic fear, successful desensitization would allow her to walk arm-in-arm with her husband among the stalactites and stalagmites.

The stop-think technique may be employed when the spouse continued to have negative ruminations about the vacation choice. If Gina were at Yellowstone Park with Gary and began to think about how hot it was, how far she was from home, and that she would like to be at the beach, she would yell subvocally, "Stop," and take from her purse an index card on which had been written positive thoughts about their being in Yellowstone, such as telling her friends that she had seen Old Faithful, and enjoying the area night life with her husband.

Selective reinforcement may involve the husband verbally and behaviorally reinforcing his wife for behaviors which manifested her enjoyment concerning the vacation choice. When Gina verbalized her astonishment at Old Faithful, Gary would move closer, put his arms around her, and tell her "You are really fun to be with." Extinction would require that Gary systematically ignore Gina's negative statements relative to their vacation choice. Statements such as "It's hot," "I wish we were home," and the like would be met with no response from Gary.

Modeling would involve the use of friends to build a more positive mental predisposition to the vacation choice. As an example, if Gary were insistent that they spend their vacation at Yellowstone Park and his wife were somewhat hesitant to do so, the counselor would instruct the wife to attempt to identify among her friends those who had visited the Park with whom she would be instructed to talk. If friends were not available, she might go to a local travel agency to get material about the vacation choice so that time and energy would become involved and invested in the impending trip.

The Premack principle may be employed by making a trip to a location of Gina's choice contingent on going to Yellowstone. A visit to the Mormon Tabernacle in Salt Lake City would be contingent on a trip to Yellowstone. In this way, Gina could look forward to their visit to the historic city while enjoying the sights of Yellowstone with her husband.

As can be seen, each of the preceding techniques is designed to improve the positive attitude of one spouse toward the vacation choice of the other which would make the entire trip more enjoyable for both. When specific techniques such as the preceding are not utilized, vacations may become nightmares. The counselor's role is one of arranging contingencies so that favorable interaction and enjoyment occur.

It should be understood that separate vacations should not occur if the first two alternatives are feasible. Spouses who spend their time away from each other do very little to increase the positive, affective component of their marriage. But when recreational interests do not overlap, spouses often agree to take separate vacations. As an example, a husband may enjoy moose hunting in Alaska, an interest not shared by his wife. Hence, the husband would board a plane with his friends and fly into the Yukon to stalk moose. Meanwhile, his wife may attend a ceramics workshop or the World's Fair with other friends. George doesn't improve his relationship with Cindy by shooting moose, just as she does not improve her relationship with George by being at the World's Fair with someone else. This is based on the premise that relationships are the result of favorable activities occurring together in time. Spouses who do not share time and space together do not value each other.

DIFFERENT HOBBIES AND INTERESTS

Spouses frequently verbalize "We don't have anything in common." When differential interests exist, the goal of therapy may become one of developing mutual hobbies and interests. This usually involves training one spouse to become more interested in an existing recreational behavior of the mate or developing a new interest for both.

In the case of the former, instruction, time together, selective reinforcement, and the Premack principle may be utilized. When a specific skill is required, such as in tennis or swimming, the spouse is enrolled in a beginner's course for that sport or is taught by the mate. When the mate is involved in the instruction of the spouse, extreme care must be taken to allow the skills of the spouse to develop very slowly. If impatience occurs, a negative attitude toward learning may result with subsequent permanent withdrawal. As an example, if Charlie is an ardent tennis player, because of his proficiency in the sport, he is likely to become impatient with his wife, Maureen, whose skills may be developing very slowly. For this reason, it is often best for the learning spouse to be enrolled in an instructional program.

When the initial skills have been acquired, the couple must specify times during which they are to enjoy the sport. This is particularly necessary since newly acquired skills must be practiced to be maintained and improved. If Maureen is learning how to play tennis, a minimum of two times each week should be allocated as tennis time. It is understood that Charlie would serve and return the ball in a way which makes it very easy for Maureen to hit it.

Selective reinforcement on the part of Charlie would be crucial in assisting Maureen in the development of her new skills. Frequent phrases such as "That was a good serve," "That was a good return," "A good backhand," etc., would result in strengthening the probability that those behaviors would recur, thereby improving Maureen's skill. It should be understood that Charlie would initially and continually reinforce any improvement, and later make reinforcement contingent on the development of greater skills.

In order to establish initial interest in a hobby or sport, the Premack principle may be utilized whereby enjoyable behaviors would be made contingent on involvement in the desired hobby or sport. As an example, Maureen may make eating and use of the phone contingent on her taking tennis lessons or playing tennis with her husband twice weekly. When the Premack principle is used consistently, it results in increasing the probability of the desired behavior occurring. Maureen would probably go without food and phone for a maximum of one day before beginning tennis instruction.

When new mutual interests are to be developed, each of the preceding techniques may be used to assist both partners in developing skills and interests in the desired activities. The development of mutual interests is often a better choice than training one spouse since the couple may learn and grow together without waiting for one spouse to catch up. Where a couple wanted to learn to ice skate, they might jointly become involved in an instructional program, spend specified periods of time practicing, selectively reinforce each other for improvement, and use the Premack principle to insure that the training sessions and time together occurred.

Happiness in marriage is not dependent on spousal agreement in all areas. A husband may become annoyed at his wife who shows little or no interest in his crops, stocks, or fish. In the same way, a wife may brood over the lack of enthusiasm her husband displays for her Green Stamp books or antiques. The erroneous cognition which creates unnecessary frustration of self and spouse is: "My spouse should think and feel as I do."

It is not unusual for a husband and wife to have different interests which do not excite, but bore, the partner. Where there is no inclination to develop the interests of the partner, a spouse may agree to accept the other's interests without participation. The spouse is encouraged to perceive the partner's hobbies and interests as enjoyable for him (her) and contingencies are established to maintain that perspective. As an example, the husband would reward his wife verbally and non-verbally (take her out to eat) when she encouraged him to go fishing and to "bring back some big ones."

12. children

Children are inextricably involved in the marital relationship. A couple recently noted that if they did not have their children, they would not have marital problems. Such a statement is an oversimplification, but bears a thread of truth, since frustrations which occur in parental roles often color the interaction in conjugal roles. The counselor may often focus on specific parent-child problems, alone or in combination with other marital difficulties.

The use of behavior modification in the parent-child relationship has been detailed by Patterson and Gullion (1968), and Madsen and Madsen (1971). These writers have identified specific behavioral problems of children and have indicated how the behavioral counselor conceptualizes and treats these difficulties. The following is expressly concerned with the marital relationship as it is affected by children, rather than specific behavioral problems of children.

NUMBER OF CHILDREN

Recently, in the waiting room of a general hospital, a young male was overheard to say, "I don't ever want no more children." On an earlier occasion a wife said, "I want a house full." Couples often disagree over the number of children they want. Behavioral treatment begins by ascertaining from the respective spouses how many children they want. The spouses usually have a firm opinion which is verbalized in the form of "none," "three," "four," or whatever. Since the number of desired children is a value decision, the couple must decide and define their values relative to their relationship. If Ann wants two children, and Phil refuses to have any, Ann must rank her values of marriage and children. If she values having children more than her marriage, she will terminate the marriage.

If Ann chooses to maintain her marriage even though children will not be planned, the counselor may focus on increasing her tolerance for being childless. Desensitization, modeling, selective reinforcement, substitutes, and cognitive dissonance may be utilized to assist her in developing a more favorable attitude toward childlessness. Desensitization may be employed by having Ann arrange in a hierarchal sequence the description of specific events which result in anxiety for her. The events would be arranged from the items of least to those of greatest anxiety. An item of considerable anxiety may be visiting her sister who just had a baby, whereas an item of low intensity may be strolling by the baby foods in the grocery store. She would then be trained how to relax, and the hierarchal scenes would be presented by the counselor.

Modeling may involve Ann spending time with wives who are childless by choice. Concurrently, Ann would be trained by modeling after the counselor to extinguish the meddling behavior of her friends and relatives concerning her childlessness. As an example, should Ann's sister ask her when she is going to have children, Ann would reply, "I don't want to discuss that." This response would eventually extinguish her sister's inquisitive behavior.

Selective reinforcement may be used by Phil who would indicate to Ann throughout the year his pleasure in their being childless. This could be done by their going on spontaneous week-end trips and his reminding Ann that these enjoyable ventures would not be possible with young children.

The purchase of a pet may be appropriate since Ann would have an outlet for some of her maternal behaviors. Ostensibly, some women would find an animal a repulsive substitute for a child, whereas others may find a plump Persian cat delightful.

Cognitive dissonance may involve Ann systematically reading about the advantages of being childless, and the problems of parenthood, with its resultant negative effect on marriage. In this way, her cognitions may become more consistent with her behavior (being childless).

In those situations in which the wife is adamant about having a child and the husband is neutral, treatment would focus on making the husband more positive in his attitude toward children. Cognitive dissonance, the Premack principle, selective reinforcement, and modeling may be useful in creating such an attitude.

Cognitive dissonance and the Premack principle may be used in combination by having the husband read favorable articles relative to childrearing and parenthood and discuss the merits of rearing a family with his wife, thereby increasing the probability of his achieving a positive attitude toward having children. In addition, positive, pleasurable activities, such as fishing and golfing, would be made contingent on the systematic discussion of his reading with his wife.

In conjunction with the above, the wife might selectively reinforce her husband for reading about and discussing parenthood with her. Hence, Everett learns that Nancy's kind behaviors, both verbal and nonverbal, are the result of his positive attitude toward a family.

Modeling may involve Everett spending time with his male friends who enjoy children and who verbalize positive feelings for them. In this way, Everett may be influenced toward more positive interaction with children and be more willing to have them.

As can be seen, each of these techniques may be utilized to develop more positive, adaptive cognitions, attitudes, and feelings concerning the number of children in a marriage. As noted earlier, the creative counselor may use other combinations or develop other techniques to achieve the goals of his clients.

SPACING OF CHILDREN

Spacing refers to when children are to be born. It is implied that spacing is an alternative available to parents. Parents who do not want to have children may use, alone or in combination, the various methods of contraception—pill, IUD, diaphragm plus spermicidal cream, condom plus foam, or cervical cap. Parents who say they are concerned about when children are conceived and who do not take contraceptive precautions should be aware of the probabilities of conceiving with unprotected exposure. In many situations, the wife wants children spaced at shorter intervals than the husband. A typical example is the wife who would like to have a child every two years, while her husband would prefer a four-year interval.

As in most marital problems, values must be specified. The wife would decide on a 10-point continuum how much she values having children every two years. She should also identify on another 10-point continuum her values relative to her marriage. In this way, the wife's values concerning her desire to space children and her desire to maintain the marriage are specified. If she desires to space children at two-year intervals at a level of 10 and to maintain her marriage at a level of 3, when these values conflict, the marriage may terminate.

The husband should also identify his values in regard to spacing the children. A husband who values his marriage at a level of 8 and his desire to space children at four-year intervals at a level of 5 will remain in the marriage if children are born every two years.

In the preceding example, treatment would focus on increasing the tolerance of the husband for children at two-year intervals. Specific techniques may include cognitive dissonance, the Premack principle, covert reinforcement, modeling, and systematic desensitization. Cognitive dissonance may involve the husband reading journal articles, magazines, and books which stress the importance of having children at short intervals. In addition, the husband would be asked to write an essay from his reading on the merits of rearing children together with positive, desirable activities contingent on his memorizing these merits and reciting them at specified intervals. As an example, on his way to fish, the husband would summarize for himself the merits of spacing children at short intervals (Premack principle).

Covert reinforcement may involve the husband thinking about desirable behaviors, such as the coming vacation, subsequent to his recalling the merits of spacing children at short intervals. Modeling may involve the husband spending time with male friends who had favorable attitudes toward child spacing at short intervals. In this way, the husband would be surrounded by people who reflect values more consistent with his desired values.

In those cases where extreme anxiety resulted from the thought of spacing children at short intervals, systematic desensitization may be employed by training the husband to relax, drawing up a hierarchy of items ranging from those eliciting the least to the greatest anxiety, and pairing these cognitions with relaxation. The successful result would enable the husband to discuss the merits of short interval spacing with his wife without anxiety.

For some couples, it may be more appropriate to identify a compromise between the spacing desires of the wife and the husband and use each of the techniques discussed to assist both spouses in developing a more favorable attitude toward the agreed upon compromise. As an example, the techniques of cognitive dissonance, the Premack principle, covert reinforcement, modeling, and desensitization may be used to assist the couple in the previous example in developing a favorable attitude toward spacing their children at three-year intervals.

DISCIPLINE OF CHILDREN

Treating couples who disagree on how their children are to be disciplined necessitates the identification and specification of what behaviors are to be disciplined, when the consequences are to be administered, and by whom.

The first area of disagreement is concerned with what behaviors are to be disciplined. This assumes that the spouses have defined what specific behaviors they want their child to learn. As an example, Jean would like for their daughter Lynn to say "Yes ma'am," whereas Neil would like Lynn to say just "Yes." Also, Neil may not want Lynn to talk when they are riding in the car, while Jean may not object to this.

In treating a couple who disagree over what the child is to be taught, the husband and wife must identify on 10-point continuums their respective values relative to disciplining their child for that specific behavior and maintaining the relationship with the spouse. As an example, Jean must decide how important it is to her that Lynn say "Yes ma'am" if this value conflicts with maintaining her marriage. If she values her marriage at a level of 3 and teaching Lynn a particular behavior at a level of 8, and if Neil is unwilling to compromise, the marriage will terminate.

In the same way, Neil would state his values relative to his desire to teach Lynn specific behaviors and his desire to maintain the marriage if these two values conflict. If he believes that his marriage is more important than teaching Lynn to say "Yes" rather than "Yes ma'am," the treatment would focus on increasing his tolerance for his daughter saying "Yes ma'am." The above may appear to be a very trivial example if it resulted in the termination of the marriage. However, value decisions relative to what behaviors the children are to learn must be specified and identified to alleviate existing difficulty and obviate future discipline problems. Although most couples will agree to compromise, some will not.

In treating the more tolerant spouse, desensitization, modeling, and contingency structuring may be employed. Desensitization would involve Neil drawing up a hierarchy of items ranging from those of lowest anxiety to those of greatest anxiety concerning Lynn's verbal behavior toward adults. The counselor would then train him to relax and pair the items on his hierarchy with relaxation. The hopeful result would be that Neil would not experience anxiety when, in his presence, his daughter responded to an adult with "Yes ma'am."

Modeling may be employed by Neil spending time with fathers whose children were taught to respond to adults with "Yes sir" and "No sir" instead of "Yes" and "No." In this way, the favorable attitude of Neil's friends toward their children's responses to adults may influence Neil positively.

A contingency may be established by having Neil place favorable, adaptive behaviors contingent on Lynn's saying "Yes, ma'am." In this way, he could earn fishing privileges by his daughter engaging in this particular verbal behavior.

Couples also disagree on when discipline is to be administered. It is probably best for discipline to be administered immediately following the behavior. Wives who tell their children, "Wait until your father gets home," are not providing an immediate consequence for the behavior just exhibited and hence, may exercise very little control over that behavior. As an example, Lynn sticks her tongue out at Jean and is not punished immediately. Lynn then is good until her father comes home. If he punishes her on his return, he will be punishing her for good behavior. Children will learn what they are taught. The father who punishes good behavior simply decreases the probability of that behavior recurring. Accordingly, the spouses are instructed to punish or reward the behavior of their children immediately or make their children clearly aware of what behavior is being punished or rewarded. The "who" of discipline is often related to the "when," since the wife frequently wants the husband to administer punishment. To reiterate, it is best if consequences follow behaviors immediately, whether these consequences are positive or negative. When Lynn throws the beach ball in the house, the parent who is present should immediately require the child to stay alone in her room for thirty minutes. In addition, phone privileges could be suspended.

It is crucial that children be rewarded for appropriate behavior, as well as their being ignored or punished for inappropriate behavior. Couples who have "bad" children have taught them to be that way, since children only learn what they are taught.

TIME WITH CHILDREN

Some spouses disagree over how much time the mate should spend with their children. A wife may feel that her husband should spend an hour a day with the children, whereas the husband may feel that spending time with the children during the week is unnecessary since he spends time with them on week-ends. Behavioral treatment would involve specifying a compromise (thirty minutes) and selecting from the techniques of modeling, selective reinforcement, desensitization, the Premack principle, and others, to achieve a more positive attitude by both spouses toward the compromise time. (It should be understood that spouses who are unwilling to compromise place the burden of change exclusively on the mate.)

Modeling may require the husband to interact with males who spend some time daily with their children and who have a favorable attitude about doing so. In the same way, the wife would be encouraged to

104

spend time with wives who were positive in their attitudes toward their husbands spending only a small amount of time with their children.

Selective reinforcement would necessitate the husband reinforcing his wife, verbally and behaviorally, for non-nagging behavior when he spent only thirty minutes daily with the children. Hence, after playing with the children for thirty minutes, Mike would tell Susan he appreciated her encouraging him to spend time with the children and being a good sport about the thirty-minute compromise. In addition, he would ask her what movie she wanted to see the following week-end. Also, Susan would tell Mike that she appreciated his playing with the children daily and that she thought he was a good father for their children. She might then tell him about the sale on golf clubs she saw at Sears. In this way, each spouse is being reinforced for a behavior which meets some of the needs of the spouse.

Systematic desensitization may be employed by desensitizing Susan to Mike's not playing with the children for one hour. She would draw up a hierarchy of items ranging from the least to the greatest in anxiety, would be trained to relax, and while relaxed, would be presented the situations on her hierarchy by the counselor. As an example, an item low on her hierarchy would be Mike's playing with the children forty-five minutes, whereas an item higher on her hierarchy would be Mike's going fishing on Saturday without playing with the children.

Mike would not be desensitized to feelings of guilt for not playing with his children for one hour, but would be instructed to play with them for only thirty minutes daily at which time he would give them his full attention. In this way, Mike would obviate the feeling of guilt for not spending one hour with his children by reminding himself when the feelings occurred that he was spending some time with his children daily.

A contingency may be employed by placing the pleasurable behaviors for Susan and Mike contingent on Mike's engagement in thirty minutes of on-task interaction with the children. Susan could earn the privileges of shopping and using the phone, while Mike could earn the privileges of smoking and fishing by his spending only thirty minutes daily with the children.

As can be seen, treatment is designed to move the partners closer together by achieving a meaningful compromise and to assist them in developing a positive attitude toward the compromise. The issues of power and control between the spouses are avoided. Hence, Susan and Mike are encouraged not to discuss whether one partner is controlling the other, but, rather, to reinforce each other and earn enjoyable privileges by both engaging in compromise behavior.

ACTIVITIES CHILD SHOULD BECOME INVOLVED IN

Most spouses are very concerned that their children do not become involved in activities which may harm them. Spouses may disagree over whether their child should be allowed to play football, spend the night in the woods, have a gun, or ride a motorcycle. The list of disagreements may be endless. Behavioral treatment will insist that the spouses specify their values relative to the activities they feel that their children should become involved in and relative to the maintenance of their marriage.

If Lydia and Barton disagree over their son's riding a motorcycle, Lydia would specify on a 10-point continuum how much she was opposed to his riding a motorcycle and on another continuum indicate how much she valued maintaining their marriage if the above value could not be achieved. In the same way, the husband would indicate on a 10-point continuum how much he was in favor of his son riding a motorcycle and on another continuum, how much he valued the marriage if the two values came into conflict. In a typical situation, the wife would rank her no motorcycle value at a level of 10 and her willingness to stay in the marriage at a level of 8, whereas the husband would rank his yes motorcycle value at a level of 10 and his marriage at a level of 7. If no compromise were possible (scooter-bike or go cart) the techniques of modeling, desensitization, involvement with motorcycle, selective reinforcement, and the Premack principle may be employed to increase the tolerance of Lydia for her son's riding a motorcycle.

Modeling may involve Lydia associating with mothers who have favorable attitudes toward their sons' riding motorcycles. In this way, Lydia may be influenced toward a more adaptive attitude concerning motorcycles.

Desensitization may be employed by Lydia drawing up a hierarchy of situations, training her to relax, and pairing the two. In this way, without anxiety, Lydia would be able to think about Robert riding the motorcycle sixty miles per hour down the highway.

Personal involvement with the motorcycle would result in Robert taking Lydia on short motorcycle trips which would be perceived as being helpful from Lydia's viewpoint. Hence, Robert may take his mother to the post office or drugstore while exercising extreme caution.

Selective reinforcement may involve Robert and Barton noticing the non-nagging behavior of Lydia concerning Robert's motorcycle riding. Robert might say, "Mom, I like you when you trust me on my motorcycle," just as Barton might say, "You're beginning to trust Robert more each day." The husband may accompany his verbal approval with an embrace and a statement concerning their outing on the week-end. A contingency may be established whereby Lydia would earn the privileges of sewing, shopping, and visiting the neighbors contingent on Robert's motorcycle riding.

Each of the above may be used in combination with Lydia selectively reinforcing Robert for safe motorcycle behavior. Hence, Robert's motorcycle time may be contingent on going at slow speeds, using hand signals, and keeping the brake system in excellent condition. To the degree Lydia believes that Robert is cautious when riding his motorcycle, she will be less anxious and more positive toward his doing so.

RIVALRY FOR CHILDREN'S LOVE

Competition between parents for their child's affection has meaning only when it is defined in terms of specific behaviors. Rivalry for the child's love is usually expressed behaviorally in three ways: (1) one spouse talks negatively about the other in the presence of the child, (2) one spouse disregards instructions given previously by the mate to the child, and (3) one spouse monopolizes the time of the child. These behaviors often result in the child learning to hate both parents as the mates learn to resent each other for the hatred instilled in the child.

After the spouses have achieved more positive, adaptive behaviors toward each other, behavioral treatment would proceed by dealing with the parent-child relationship. Having dealt with the interaction of the spouses, the parent-child problem regarding rivalry for love may have disappeared. On the other hand, unadaptive habit systems may have been developed which may be difficult to break. When one spouse talks negatively about the other, the Premack principle, selective reinforcement, and modeling may be used in combination. In using the Premack principle, the wife would be instructed to record the number of positive and negative statements she said daily to Billie about Fred, and her enjoyable activities would be made contingent on these positive statements. Each positive statement Joyce made to Billie about Fred would earn one point which Joyce could exchange for the privilege of smoking one cigarette. In addition, each negative statement would cost Joyce three

Treatment should focus initially on the relationship of the spouses independent of the child. Since one or both spouses is undermining the other through the child, specific behavioral referents that resulted in dislike for the spouse are sought and identified. As an example, Joyce may tell Billie, their child, that Fred is a bad man because he is always drinking and never at home. The counselor would first treat Fred's drinking and the amount of time the couple spend with each other in an effort to increase their mutual emotional and physical affection. The specific problems of drinking, late behavior, and time together would be treated as outlined earlier prior to parent-child interaction.

cigarettes. The program would enable Joyce to earn smoking privileges very quickly initially, whereas later, more points would be required for each cigarette. Hence, initially, one point would be necessary for one cigarette, whereas a week later, five points may be necessary. This initial rapid point accumulation is an effort to allow the client to earn privileges as quickly as possible, while producing observable, desired behavior.

Selective reinforcement would involve Fred's verbally and behaviorally rewarding Joyce for observable improvement as indexed by her log sheets. If Joyce logged more positive interaction today than yesterday, Fred would say, "You are really serious about improving," which would be accompanied by an embrace and a statement that they should go out to get ice cream or take a short ride. Modeling may involve Joyce's spending time with friends who interact positively with their children and who make positive statements about their husbands to their children.

Rivalry for the child's love is often manifested by a disregard on the part of one spouse for the previous instructions of the other to the child. One parent will allow the child to do things which the spouse has specifically instructed the child not to do. This is functional if the spouse and the child make the discrimination that a behavior is appropriate in one situation and not in another. As an example, a father does not allow his children to ask if they can buy things when they are in a dimestore, whereas he does not object if the children ask their mother. In this situation, the children make the discrimination that asking behavior is appropriate in shopping situations with mother, but not with father. These discriminations are functional. On the other hand, some spouses undermine the authority of the mate by giving the child opposite instructions and encouraging him to disobey. Fred may tell Billie that he may shoot the BB gun anytime, whereas Joyce has told Billie that he is to shoot the gun only when his father is present to oversee him.

The issue of what activities the child should become involved in should be separated from the issue of one parent undercutting the other. The former has been dealt with in the preceding paragraphs; the treatment of the latter may involve the use of the Premack principle and selective reinforcement. In the preceding situation, the counselor may ask Fred to log the number of times he made statements to Billie which counteracted the instructions given by Joyce. Having decided what behaviors Billie is to become involved in, the enjoyable activities for Fred are made contingent on being consistent with Joyce about what Billie may and may not do. Fishing and golfing for Fred would be made contingent on his saying to Billie that the BB gun should be shot only when they are together. Hence, Fred is supporting his wife rather than undermining her authority in relation to Billie. Selective reinforcement would involve Joyce verbally and behaviorally reinforcing Fred for supporting her instructions to Billie.

Rivalry for the child's love is also manifested by one spouse spending an exorbitant amount of time with the child to the exclusion of the mate. It is not unusual for the mother to spend every waking hour with the child even though the husband may be in the home much of the time. Monopolizing the child's time may involve undermining the spouse as discussed above. Specific treatment for amount of time with the child may involve programming family time and reinforcing the monopolizing spouse for spending less time with the child. Hence, if Joyce spent much of her day with Billie, a specified amount of time would be allocated during which Joyce, Fred, and Billie would recreate together. In this way, time alone with Billie would be reduced by definition. In addition, Fred may selectively reinforce Joyce for spending less time with Billie by doing things with her which require her attention and which do not involve the child. Going to the movies, bowling, and fishing together are activities which may increase the positive interpersonal relationship between the spouses while weaning Joyce from the child.

RETARDED CHILD

Happy marriages are often shattered by the birth of a retarded or malformed child. Previous analysis of data relating to families with a severely retarded or malformed child indicates two possible types of crises. The initial crisis occurs at the time the child is diagnosed as retarded or is observed to be malformed. This awareness often results in a response similar to that of bereavement since anticipated plans are often frustrated and demolished. The second type results from the inability to cope with the situation over time. In effect, the parents are unable to adjust their roles to meet the needs of the child. Farber (1960) has indicated the advisability of institutionalizing a child who is severely retarded. Ostensibly, whether or not institutionalization occurs depends on the level of retardation, professional assistance available within the community, money, and willingness of the parents to institutionalize or to work with the child. Should the parents decide to keep the child, the counselor would assist them in resolving specific behavioral problems with the child, such as toilet training, self feeding, etc.

In those cases in which the parents have decided to institutionalize the child, treatment would be designed toward decreasing the guilt of the parents for such institutionalization. Techniques such as desensitization, modeling, periodic visits, and cognitive dissonance may be useful to decrease the feelings of guilt. Desensitization would involve having the respective spouses develop hierarchies ranging from those items which created the least anxiety to those which created the most anxiety, learning to relax, and having the items paired with relaxation by the counselor. The result of successful desensitization would be the ability of both spouses to think about their child in the institutionalized setting without anxiety.

Modeling may be used by having the parents visit with parents of other institutionalized children who had adaptive, positive attitudes toward that institutionalization and who expressed a favorable attitude about same. Periodic visits would be employed initially. The parents would be expected to visit the institution, talk with the doctors and nurses, and develop some assurance that their child was being taken care of by professionals. After this initial assurance had been established, visits would become less frequent until desensitization had proceeded far enough so that they could visit without anxiety. Cognitive dissonance may be employed by having both spouses write essays and discuss with each other the advantages of institutionalization.

SEX EDUCATION AND CHILDREN

One of the deepest concerns of parents today is that their children develop and mature into functional sexual adults. By "functional sexual adults" reference is made to mature men and women who have a high positive regard for sex which, when transformed into behaviors, is consistent with the social and cultural norms of our society. In discussing sex education with parents, the counselor must make two issues clear: (1) sex education of their children will occur and (2) parents are responsible. Many parents deceive themselves by assuming that somehow if they do not talk about sex, their children will find out the right things anyway. The assumption is as tragic as it is sad. Parents who avoid teaching their children about sex are like postmen who fail to deliver the mail or firemen who sleep through alarms. In addition, parents who wait for the school to perform this function often wait too long. In a Purdue poll (1966) of 1000 teenagers, 53% of the boys and 43% of the girls indicated that sex information was taught to them by friends and other people their own age. Less than 20% of the boys and 33% of the girls were given the information by their parents. Parents are responsible for what their children learn about sex and cannot delegate that responsibility to the school, neighbor, peers, or books.

The counselor's role in discussing sex education with parents encompasses three issues: (1) teacher, (2) model, and (3) identification of specifics. Initially, the counselor will assist his clients in correcting misunderstandings they may have in regard to sex. Most parents who are hesitant to provide sex education for their children have been relying for years on sexual myths. This didactic interaction may involve the counselor suggesting that his clients read McCary (1967) and discussing with them any issues which need clarification. As the counselor discusses sex with his clients, he becomes a model for them in their discussion with their children. In a usual situation, the parents have never heard sex discussed, which increases their need for an appropriate model.

A third role of the counselor is that of identifying specifics which the parents should discuss with their children. This is preceded by a general orientation as to what sex education is. Kirkendall (1952) defined six goals of sex education which are reflective of the basic philosophy behind it: (1) sex education should help children feel that each part of the body and each phase of growth is good and has a purpose. While children should not be preoccupied with any one part of the body or its function, they should be able to talk about both part and function freely and without embarrassment. (2) Sex education should give children a clear understanding of reproductive processes. They should have the knowledge that all life comes from life and that reproduction occurs in many forms. (3) Sex education should prepare children for the changes and developments which accompany their maturation. (4) Sex education should help young people see that sexual conduct involving other persons needs to be based upon a sincere regard for the welfare of others. (5) Sex education should make children proud of their own sex and yet appreciative of the attributes and capacities of the other sex. (6) Sex education should create a feeling that sex is a positive, creative, and dignified part of life. Each of these goals is consistent with specific areas of discussion about which the counselor assists his clients in talking with their children. These specifics include: words, bodily processes, forms of sexual behavior, venereal disease, pregnancy, contraception, and boy-girl differences with respect to love and sex.

Before any discussion between parents and children may occur, basic words must be known and defined. Parents should make a list of every word which they feel their children should know and which would be relevant to a discussion of sex. Penis, vagina, clitoris, menstruation, venereal disease, contraception, gestation, masturbation, etc., should be defined explicitly with the child. Ostensibly, the counselor would suggest that the parents discuss these various terms with the children only after their anxiety is zero when doing so. In this way, a positive, non-fearful attitude toward sex would be communicated.

In the area of bodily functions, every girl should know what menstruation is; every boy should know what seminal emissions are; every child should know about the bodily functions of both sexes. Forms of sexual behavior discussed should be those of masturbation, petting, and sexual intercourse with the emphasis being that these are alternative forms of sexual expressions. In discussing these aspects of sexual behavior, the parents may choose to include their moral teachings, i.e., sexual intercourse is appropriate under some conditions, but not others, as are masturbation and petting.

The various forms of venereal disease, such as syphilis and gonorrhea, as well as various forms of contraception should be discussed. In addition, the child should fully understand the nature of conception, pregnancy, and childbirth. Ostensibly, the level of understanding should be geared to the age of the child. As an example, a five-year-old who is only concerned about why his mother has a fat stomach could be answered by "Daddy put a baby seed inside," whereas an older child may want to know the specifics of conception.

Every girl should be told that an erection may occur when she puts her hand on her boyfriend's leg, just as boys should be told that every girl may not be aware of this and it does not mean that she wants to have intercourse (Madsen, 1968). In addition, every girl should be made aware that boys often do not connect sex with love, whereas girls often do. Hence, when Johnny wants to have intercourse with Sally, this does not necessarily mean that he loves her.

In essence, the counselor's role is one of assisting the clients in becoming more comfortable personally with the discussion of sex and of providing them with specific material which they may discuss with their children. It should be understood that sex education is not relegated to a fifty-minute discussion of sex, but that the child will learn a great deal about sex by watching his parents interact emotionally, socially, and physically. On the other hand, such observation is not sufficient and direct information must be communicated.

PART THREE

APPLICATION

The value of a behavioral approach to marital happiness can only be assessed by observing changes in the behaviors of those couples who become involved in marriage counseling. Modification of behavior is the end result any marriage counselor, of whatever persuasion, hopes to see. To the extent that behavior is not modified in the desired direction, therapy has failed. The counselor should also acknowledge that while many of his clients may be improved and better able to function, some will be unchanged, and others may become worse because of his involvement. The counselor must share responsibility for all outcomes based upon his interventions and recognize when he has reached an impasse and is unable to proceed.

The abstract cases from the writer's files are in a format basic to a behavioral approach and devised by Lindsley (1966). The style does not include the "non-specifics" (Lazarus, 1968) or "placebo effect" of the client-therapist relationship, often said to be of critical importance. In addition, except in three cases, no follow-up data are reported.

Perhaps the most important, single, distinguishing characteristic of a behavioral approach is the reliance on recording of measurable and observable behavior. These case studies are based upon clients' self-report (which Simkins, 1971, ably questions) with virtually no reliability of observational data. However, when the alternatives are no data or client's data, the counselor should insist on the latter.

MARRIAGE

13. counseling

 ## CASE I
SHE CHEATED

A thirty-two year old male complained that he was insanely jealous of his wife's previous affair—her fourth. Since the wife had been repentent and promised to be faithful, the treatment goal was one of alleviating his compulsive thinking and talking about the affair.

PINPOINT:
Compulsive thoughts and negative statements about wife's previous affair.

RECORD:
"Continuous"

CONSEQUATE:

A.   THE PREMACK PRINCIPLE. The clients's job was made contingent on not verbalizing about the previous affair. Every minute he did not discuss the affair with his wife, he earned one minute of job time.

B. AVERSIVE CONSEQUENCES. Each time client mentioned affair, he was to lose one hour of time at work.

C. EXTINCTION. Should the husband bring up the affair, the wife was not to respond, but to withdraw from the room.

D. SELECTIVE REINFORCEMENT. Wife was to tell the husband when he was not discussing the affair that she liked him best when he talked about them. In addition, she was to approach him for intercourse every day that he did not discuss the affair.

E. STOP-THINK. Every time the husband thought about the affair, he was to yell "stop," get out an index card on which were written positive, pleasurable characteristics about the relationship between his wife and him, and read each card.

F. DESENSITIZATION. Desensitization was not appropriate for this client since he could neither relax nor construct a clear mental image.

EVALUATE: (1 week later)

Although the couple had jointly agreed to participate in the treatment program, the husband discussed the affair continually without subsequent job loss, while the wife did not withdraw from such discussion nor did she selectively reinforce him at times when he was not talking about the affair. The husband noted that the stop-think technique was inadequate since he would always be yelling "stop" if he used it. The writer discussed with them their values in regard to maintaining their marriage and suggested the positive consequences of their following the treatment procedures. The couple verbally reiterated their interest in maintaining the marriage and agreed to follow the treatment program, which had been devised and discussed with them.

CONSEQUATE 2:

A. When the client was about to bring up the past, he was to leave the house immediately and stay away until he no longer needed to discuss the affair. In addition, his wife could also leave if he refused to do so when the affair was mentioned.

B. If the client was unable to control his verbalizations, he was to write down everything he was about to say and to speak only from the written page. This would obviate blurting out inappropriate verbalizations.

C. The husband was to write down five things, positive in nature, that he wanted to discuss with his wife, and they were to discuss these together thirty minutes each day from 9:30 to 10:00 P.M. Positive interaction must occur if the relationship were to improve.

D. Intercourse was to occur, preceded by thirty minutes of foreplay, anytime the client wanted it, contingent on his not having talked about the affair.

EVALUATE 2: (1 week later)

The husband came to treatment alone and noted that while riding with his wife in their pick-up truck two days previously, he was ruminating again about her previous affair and began to swerve the truck, sock his wife, and yell obscenities at her. When his wife recovered, she left him. Therapy was terminated without having achieved the goals.

It is difficult to say if the goals of the client would have been accomplished had the couple followed the treatment plan specifically since he had been reinforced over the past six years for non-trusting behavior as defined by his wife's periodic affairs. However, a discussion of the client's insecurities, self-concept, and dependency needs had also resulted in no observable, positive changes—a therapeutic failure. (It is interesting to note that Wickramasekera, 1970, successfully treated a 41-year-old male who complained of restlessness, insomnia, sporadic crying, and extended outbursts of verbal abuse such as "bitch" and "whore" where such behavior was said to be a function of his wife's recent "infidelity.")

● CASE 2
DON'T TOUCH ME

The J.'s were a middle class couple. They had been married twenty-five years and had four children.

PINPOINT:

Mrs. J. experienced tension and a feeling of being pressured by her husband to have intercourse.

RECORD:

Tension occurred every time husband touched her independent of his desire for intercourse.

CONSEQUATE:

A. Mr. and Mrs. J. were not to have intercourse under any conditions for one week.

B. Three times each day, Mr. J. was to approach his wife, put his arms around her, and tell her that he loved her.

C. Independent of the above, each evening the couple were to spend thirty minutes together talking, hugging, kissing, and caressing, all of which was never to be followed by intercourse.

EVALUATE: (1 week later)

Although the couple followed the treatment plan specifically, Mrs. J. did not feel completely comfortable during sexual interaction with her husband because she felt at any moment he was going to press for intercourse.

CONSEQUATE 2:

A. The couple were to continue their thirty minute cuddle sessions.

B. Every other night, beginning the night of the interview, the couple was not to have intercourse under any circumstances (four "no" nights).

C. On each "no" night, Mrs. J. was to make herself sexually desirable (via nightgown and perfume) and beg her husband to have intercourse with her during their thirty-minute cuddle session.

D. Mr. J. was not to have intercourse with his wife on a "no" night no matter what she said or did.

E. On alternate nights, intercourse could take place only if Mrs. J. said, "I really want you to." This was the only condition under which intercourse could take place in the next week.

Consequate 2 was a continued attempt to make Mrs. J. more comfortable in sexual interaction with her husband by programming specific times in which intercourse could not take place under any conditions, and others in which intercourse could occur only if she specifically made a certain response. In this way, she was choosing when to have intercourse, thus alleviating the pressure to have intercourse when she did not choose to do so. At the same time, she was also learning that Mr. J. was not always sexually available to her since specific times had been programmed in which nothing she did would result in her husband having intercourse with her.

EVAULATE 2: (1 week later)

The couple indicated that intercourse had occurred four times during the last week (all on "no" nights). Both indicated verbally and behaviorally positive feelings toward the other. Mr. J. indicated that he was not able to resist his wife's sexual approaches.

CONSEQUATE 3:

A. The counselor reiterated to Mr. J. the importance of refusing his wife for intercourse since she would only learn that he could refuse by his exhibiting that behavior. Mr. J. stated firmly that he could refuse his wife at any time he chose to and placed a twenty-dollar bet that he would be able to do so.

B. Mrs. J. was instructed to approach her husband for intercourse four times the following week, with Mr. J. refusing intercourse the first time and once of the remaining three.

C. Each intercourse was to be preceded by thirty minutes of foreplay.

EVALUATE 3: (1 week later)

Treatment plan was followed specifically. Mrs. J. experienced no tension or feeling of pressure in sexual interaction with her husband. Therapy was terminated with the instructions that she continue to approach him three times weekly and for him to refuse her on a one-to-three ratio.

A nine-month follow-up indicated a continued mutual enjoyment and a heightened state of marital happiness for both partners.

● CASE 3
PARAPLEGIC

Mr. and Mrs. H. had been married for twenty-three years, had five children and lived in a small midwestern town. Mr. H. had multiple sclerosis and for one year had not had an erection. Mrs. H. noted that their sex life had deteriorated to nothing and was seriously impairing their marriage. The husband enjoyed manually manipulating his wife, but she did not enjoy this because orgasm did not follow. As a result, Mrs. H. continually withdrew from her husband's incessant approaches.

PINPOINT:

Wife refused husband's approaches.

RECORD:

Five refusals each week.

CONSEQUATE:

Mrs. H. was to approach her husband three times weekly for manual stimulation by him which was to be accompanied by the use of an electric vibrator.

EVALUATE: (1 week later)

Husband was satisfied and happy with wife's approaches and wife enjoyed stimulation which resulted in orgasm. A continued treatment program was established whereby Mrs. H.'s church attendance was contingent on her approaching her husband three times weekly, and Mr. H.'s cigar smoking was contingent on his not approaching his wife. (Behavioral treatment was not directed toward Mr. H's impotence since his physician indicated to the counselor that his condition was irreparable).

● CASE 4
I'M IMPOTENT

The S. couple had been married for twenty-four years and had three children. They lived in one of the larger Eastern cities. Mr. S. was referred by a psychiatrist.

PINPOINT:
Mr. S. had been unable to create and maintain an erection.

RECORD:
An erection had occurred once every three months for the past twelve years.

CONSEQUATE:

A. The couple were not to have intercourse under any conditions during the next week.

B. Two thirty-minute time periods were designated in which they would talk, cuddle, kiss, and caress both with and without their clothes on.

C. Mr. S. was to discover ways in which he could satisfy his wife other than penile vaginal penetration, such as manual stimulation or oral-genital relations.

EVALUATE: (1 week later)
The couple followed the treatment plan with no erection resulting. In addition, Mrs. S. experienced considerable anxiety and a negative attitude toward her husband stimulating her manually and orally.

CONSEQUATE 2:

A. The couple was instructed to purchase an electric vibrator and the husband was instructed in its use.

B. No intercourse was to occur during the next week.

C. Mr. S. was to use the vibrator on his wife three times.

D. Cuddle time was to continue with Mr. S. rating the degree of anxiety experienced on a 10-point continuum.

E. Mrs. S. was to recall specific times in which Mr. S. had created and maintained an erection, and discuss these with husband during their cuddle time. These were events in which they had enjoyed sex together and in which Mr. S. had performed successfully.

F.   Mrs. S. was to log the number of positive statements which she said about sex, as well as the number of negative statements, and bring her log to therapy.

EVALUATE 2: (1 week later)
During the week Mr. S. experienced a very strong erection which resulted in an "uncontrollable" desire to have intercourse with subsequent orgasms for both partners.

CONSEQUATE 3:
A.   They were to engage in thirty minutes of foreplay and were to use the vibrator every other time with Mrs. S. achieving orgasm first through the use of the vibrator and then Mr. S. achieving orgasm through intercourse if he chose to do so.

B.   Every other time Mr. S. had an erection, regardless of how stiff, he was to allow his penis to become flaccid and begin again if he so chose.

C.   Mrs. S. was to reinforce him systematically and positively each time he experienced or approximated an erection.

EVALUATE 3: (4 weeks later)
Erections occurred at will.

● CASE 5
I'M FRIGID—HE EJACULATES TOO QUICKLY
Mr. and Mrs. G. had been married for two years. Mrs. G. had previously been diagnosed as "frigid," and her husband complained of premature ejaculation. Since the marital relationship, excluding the sexual difficulties, was reported to be one of extreme happiness, the presented problems became the focus of treatment.

PINPOINT:
Wife did not experience orgasm.

RECORD:
Never.

CONSEQUATE:
A general discussion of sex, as outlined in Chapter Four in regard to the behaviors of sex and the alternate meanings of intercourse, preceded directions to alleviate the problem of "frigidity":

A. Following a discussion designed to ascertain the advisability of recommending the vibrator (see Appendix), the couple was instructed to purchase an inexpensive model and to use it during the next week.

B. They were to buy the current issue of **Sexology** magazine and discuss with each other the specific articles they read. Discussing articles on sex was designed to provide a cognitive loosening experience.

EVALUATE: (1 week later)
A pleasurable orgasm was experienced by Mrs. G. through the use of the vibrator.

CONSEQUATE 2:
The vibrator was to be used three times in the next week.

EVALUATE 2: (1 week later)
The vibrator was used three times since the last meeting and resulted in an extremely pleasant orgasm one time, a "baby" orgasm the second time, and no orgasm the third. It was explained that there are times that the vibrator will not produce an orgasm, although if it is used consistently, it will produce a climactic experience 85–95% of the time.

At this point, the focus of treatment shifted from Mrs. G., who was now experiencing pleasurable sexual feelings in sexual interaction with her husband, to Mr. G. and his problem of premature ejaculation. In this particular case, Mr. G. was elated that his wife did experience orgasms even though they were not in direct response to intercourse with him.

PINPOINT:
Premature ejaculation

RECORD:
Ejaculation occurred within one to five seconds after every penetration.

CONSEQUATE:
A. On one occasion, Mrs. G. was to manually manipulate her husband until he experienced a feeling of approaching ejaculation at a tension level of seven, which he would communicate to her by squeezing her arm. She was then to stop and begin again when he indicated his level had subsided to zero. She was to repeat the process for five times, the last including ejaculation.

B. On two other occasions, the following was to occur:

1. Mr. G. was to engage in fifteen minutes of foreplay with Mrs. G.;
2. Mr. G. was then to penetrate and withdraw before ejaculation;
3. They were to use the vibrator on Mrs. G. until orgasm;
4. Mr. G. was to penetrate until his orgasm.

An attempt was being made to increase the threshold of anxiety for Mr. G., while at the same time, associating penile vaginal penetration with the vibrator for Mrs. G. since the penis preceded the vibrator. In addition, penetration to ejaculation was to occur after Mrs. G. had had an orgasm, thus reducing the tension of Mr. G. to delay his ejaculation to produce an orgasm in Mrs. G.

EVALUATE: (1 week later)
Although his successes were sporadic, Mr. G. experienced a gradual increase in his ability to delay ejaculation. At one point, he delayed ejaculation for four minutes of sustained stimulation.

CONSEQUATE 2:
Mr. G. was to think about competing thoughts while being manipulated by his wife. Since he was a tennis enthusiast, he was to mentally keep score in a game with his most ardent competitor. In addition, he was to think about working at his place of employment and having a consultation with his boss. Ostensibly, these were behaviors which require considerable concentration.

EVALUATE 2: (1 week later)
Mr. G.'s ability to delay ejaculation continued to increase, although sporadically. On one occasion, he delayed ejaculation for twenty minutes.

CONSEQUATE 3:
An attempt was made to increase the delay of ejaculation.
A. Mrs. G. was not to allow her husband to see her naked prior to intercourse.
B. She was to wear a non-see-through blouse while having intercourse and Mr. G. was not to attempt to "peek" under or below the blouse.
C. They were to talk before and during intercourse. This was crucial in that presumably talking and thinking inhibited sexual anxiety for Mr. G.
D. Mrs. G. was not to move her body toward her husband, touch him, etc., until after he ejaculated.
E. The sequence of their sexual interaction was to be as outlined in Consequate 1.

EVALUATE 3: (1 week later)

Mr. G. delayed ejaculation while having intercourse an average of eleven minutes during their three periods of intercourse the previous week, one time delaying for twenty-five minutes. (Comment: Masters' and Johnson's "squeeze technique" for treating premature ejaculation became known to the writer after this couple had terminated therapy. Their research indicates that their procedure is most efficacious and should be used as the treatment of choice for premature ejaculation.)

● CASE 6
HOW COULD SHE?

This upper middle class couple, living in one of the larger metropolitan areas, had been married for twelve years and had two children. Mrs. R., a secretary, lost her job over an alleged affair with one of the employees. Her husband believed that she was not involved in an affair, but noted that she might have been.

PINPOINT:

Husband verbalized to wife that she would not have lost her job if she and the fellow employee had been on-task.

RECORD:

One-third of Mr. R.'s statements to his wife were in reference to the alleged affair.

CONSEQUATE:

A. Every five minutes Mr. R. did not verbalize statements about the alleged affair, Mrs. R. was to look at him and say to him, "John, I like being with you when you are this way." She was to do this every five minutes for the first day.

B. On subsequent days, Mrs. R. was to "catch" Mr. R. being positive every ten minutes and to express her approval with kisses and other forms of physical affection. Hence, Mr. R. would get affection and attention contingent on his non-nagging behavior.

C. Mr. R. was to count the number of minutes that he was positive while around Mrs. R. and make his smoking contingent on positive interaction. Every five minutes of positive interaction would earn him one cigarette. (Mr. R. smoked two packs daily.)

EVALUATE: (1 week later)

Neither Mr. or Mrs. R. engaged in the treatment behaviors. They described their relationship as unchanged.

CONSEQUATE 2:

Mr. R. was to go into the garage and stay for thirty minutes contingent on his mentioning the previous affair.

EVALUATE 2: (1 week later)

No change. Mr. R. said that he had a compulsion to talk about the affair.

CONSEQUATE 3:

A.   Mr. R. was to write down every word or phrase he was about to say to Mrs. R., and decide if each was positive before speaking.

B.   Smoking and intercourse were made contingent on positive statements to Mrs. R. Hence, every day negative verbalizations did not occur, Mrs. R. would approach her husband for intercourse. In addition, smoking privileges could be earned by making positive statements.

C.   They were to spend fifteen minutes together daily in on-task communication from 9:00 to 9:15 P.M.

EVALUATE 3: (1 week later)

Mr. and Mrs. R. verbally and behaviorally indicated that their relationship had improved trememdously since the last meeting. Mr. R. (who had discontinued his negative statements about the affair) said that he felt that his wife was more serious about her concern for him. In the same way, Mrs. R. reiterated her love for her husband and noted that she enjoyed being around him when he talked about positive things. (Comment: The terminating interview did not seem consistent with the previous behavior of the clients. This may be attributed to the new job which Mr. R. had contracted which resulted in their moving out of the community in which the presumed affair had occurred. The last interview was characterized by such phrases as "what we will do.")

● **CASE 7**

MAKE UP YOUR MIND

Mr. W. had been involved in an affair with his secretary for five years. His wife of twelve years became aware of his affair and pleaded with him to see a marriage counselor. They had three daughters. Mr. W. said that he loved both his mistress and his wife and could not decide what to do. The W's lived in a large city in the deep South.

PINPOINT:

Ambivalence concerning whether to terminate relationship with mistress or wife.

RECORD:
Mr. W. changed his mind a minimum of twice daily about which one he would stay with.

CONSEQUATE:

A. Decide to decide. Mr. W. was unwilling to terminate his ambivalence (it had been reinforced for five years).

B. Mrs. W. noted calmly, but firmly, that she wanted a decision by September 1, it then being July 15.

C. The next six weeks were spent increasing the positive behaviors of Mrs. W., discussing the various consequences of Mr. W's alternative decisions, supporting Mrs. W. during her husband's ambivalence, and preparing her for possible divorce. The clients were seen both separately and jointly.

EVALUATE: (6 weeks later)
Mr. W. announced that he had decided to leave his wife. That evening he did so.

● CASE 8
THE ETERNAL TRIANGLE

Mrs. L., an attractive, twenty-three-year old, married coed, noted that she was still in love with a former boyfriend, then in Vietnam. Although she had been separated three weeks, she reported that she had been confused for about six months concerning whom she loved. After three sessions of considering the alternatives of loving her husband versus her former boyfriend, she chose as her goal to improve the relationship with her husband.

PINPOINT:
Writing to former boyfriend and reading his letters.

RECORD:
Mrs. L. wrote one letter weekly and read his letters daily.

CONSEQUATE:

A. Mrs. L. was to burn her boyfriend's letters and return all subsequent mail unopened.

B. She was to write a letter which included the following:
    1. her decision to be faithful to her husband,
    2. her regret that they had become involved,
    3. her unwillingness to write, talk, or see him again.

C. Because of her hesitancy in terminating the relationship with her former boyfriend, a specific day, time, and place for mailing the letter was established.

(It should be clear that an improvement in the relationship with her husband was dependent on the termination of the availability of her boyfriend as a potential reinforcer.)

EVALUATE: (1 week later)
Mrs. L. did burn her former boyfriend's letters and mail the "Dear John." She reported the latter to be most difficult. (The writer verbally reinforced her for doing what she had decided to do.)

PINPOINT:
Positive thoughts and feelings for husband.

RECORD:
One a week.

CONSEQUATE:
At this point, Mrs. L.'s husband became involved in therapy and was made aware of his wife's dissatisfactions. He was cooperative in modifying his behaviors consistent with her expectations (probably the turning point in therapy). In addition, Mrs. L. was instructed (while husband was absent from therapy room) to make a list of five things her husband would like for her to do each day and to do them. Some specific examples included taking her husband's watch to the jeweler, making a chocolate pound cake, and serving him his favorite wine after dinner. (This technique has been extremely useful in inducing a more positive attitude toward the love object. It assumes that we come to love those with whom we invest time and effort.)

EVALUATE: (3 weeks later)
Mrs. L. reported that she had been able to return two letters to her former boyfriend and that she and her husband had enjoyed themselves at the beach. She had decided to move back in with him the previous week.

One year follow-up revealed a verbalized, continued, mutual enjoyment and the presence of a baby daughter via adoption.

● CASE 9
HE IGNORES ME
Mrs. P. had been married for twenty-seven years and had three children. Her husband did not accompany her to the interview.

PINPOINT:
Husband ignored wife.

RECORD:
Husband in fact did not ignore wife as defined by his calling her every time he was out of town (three days weekly). In addition, he depended on her to go with him to social events, bridge parties, etc.

CONSEQUATE:
A. The behavioral alternatives for Mrs. P. were made clear:
   1. remain in the relationship and improve it with the husband's participation,
   2. adjust to the relationship without Mr. P.'s participation.
   3. terminate the relationship.
   Since Mrs. P. said she had "no place to go," termination was not an acceptable alternative.
B. To assist her in increasing the probability of her husband's approach and attention behavior, Mrs. P. was instructed to identify those situations in which her husband depended on her and to withdraw from them. As an example, when her husband was out of town and called her one evening, she was instructed not to answer the phone. The case history noted that Mr. P. always wanted Mrs. P. when she was not available. To withdraw her as a reinforcer might increase her reinforcement value for him. She was also to reward his "at home" approach behavior.
C. Mrs. P. was instructed to identify other sources of potential reinforcement, such as her job, friends, and volunteer work. In this way, she could lessen her dependence on her husband.

EVALUATE: (2 weeks later)
Mrs. P. canceled her next appointment without explanation. Many clients come to therapy and discover that value decisions should be made and new behaviors should be instigated to achieve their goals. This revelation may result in dropping from therapy. In Mrs. P.'s case, it is probable that she decided that she would continue to tolerate her husband's indifference and canceled the appointment.

● CASE 10
THE BUSINESS
Mr. and Mrs. B. had been married ten years and had two children. Mrs. B. complained that her husband was completely absorbed psychologically, emotionally, and physically in his job to the exclusion of interaction with

her and their children. She noted that if such absorption continued she would be unwilling to remain in the relationship. Mr. B. agreed that the time he spent with his business was excessive and was willing to do something about it.

PINPOINT:
Husband spends too little time with spouse and children.

RECORD:
Zero

CONSEQUATE:

A. They were to spend thirty minutes each evening together in on-task interaction. For the first fifteen minutes, Mr. B. was to ask direct questions to his wife, such as how was her day, the children, etc. He was then to discuss with her anything he chose, which could involve his business. In addition, they were mutually to reveal some of their inner feelings about themselves, the other partner, and their relationship.

B. Mr. B. was to spend fifteen minutes alone each evening thinking about the very worst things that could possibly happen to his business. He was to imagine reading in the **Wall Street Journal** that all the companies in which he had stock had gone bankrupt. In addition, he was to think about the fact that his business had burned and what he would do should this occur.

C. Mr. and Mrs. B. were to go somewhere, e.g., restaurant, shopping, etc. and spend a block of time (six hours) together each weekend, with him deciding where they would go and what they would do.

EVALUATE: (1 week later)
The husband did not engage in any of the behaviors specified in the treatment program.

CONSEQUATE 2:
As a result, his wife decided that they would separate and that she would call a lawyer the next morning. Mr. B. unwillingly noted that he would move out of the home and find an apartment. The decision for Mr. B. to leave was one which resulted from his wife's unwillingness to tolerate his continued apathy. There seemed to be considerable compassion on the part of one for the other with little overt hostility.

EVALUATE 2: (1 week later)
The husband did not move out, but began to engage in the specific

behaviors outlined in treatment, i.e., time with wife, children, and
week-end events. The wife noted that she was very happy with her
husband and that as long as he spent time with them, she wanted him to
stay. (His remaining in the home was made contingent on spending time
with his wife and children.)

● CASE 11
I WANT TO FISH

Mr. and Mrs. D. had been married for twelve years and had four children.
Mrs. D. complained that her husband spent too much time fishing and that
if he did not stop, she would terminate the marriage. Her value on a
10-point continuum for his fishing was zero and her willingness to
maintain the marriage if he did not terminate his fishing was also zero. On
the other hand, Mr. D. said that he valued fishing at a level of 9, but that
he would choose to maintain the marriage at a level of 10 if these values
came into conflict.

PINPOINT:
Fishing behavior of husband.

RECORD:
Twice weekly

CONSEQUATE:
Spouse would divorce him if fishing occurred again.

EVALUATE: (1 week later)
Husband did not fish, but spent that time with his wife. This resulted in
Mrs. D. feeling guilty about depriving her husband from fishing and made
her more willing to discuss her husband's fishing in moderation. Moderate
fishing was defined as fishing five times per month, with a maximum of
two fishing trips any given week and an agreement that these could not be
accumulated one month for use the next month. In addition, Mrs. D. was
also concerned that he spend some time with her and the children and that
he be home from fishing at a specified time.

CONSEQUATE 2:
Husband could fish five times monthly as specified above, with weekly
fishing privileges contingent on being home by 8:00 P.M. or calling
beforehand. In addition, the couple were to spend one afternoon weekly
together engaging in behavior which they both enjoyed, such as golfing.

EVALUATE: (1 week later)

The couple followed the treatment behaviors specifically and noted an observable increase in their marital happiness. What initially appeared to be a very poor marriage as defined by Mrs. D.'s ultimatum resulted in behavioral changes by her husband and subsequent changes in Mrs. D. The probabilities of marital happiness are increased when expectations and contingencies are made clear.

●CASE 12
EVERYTHING IS WRONG

Few marital problems are single-dimensional. Rather, there is usually an array of difficulties experienced by the spouses. Treatment consists of identifying each of the specific problem areas and consequenting each behavior. When problems are multi-dimensional, it is impossible to correct them by setting one major contingency. The case to follow reports the treatment of an upper middle class couple who had been married for fifteen years. Mr. and Mrs. C. had three children.

PINPOINT:
The couple did not spend time together.

RECORD:
On-task time together never occurred.

CONSEQUATE:
They were to spend thirty minutes together daily in on-task interaction. This time was specified as being between 9:30 and 10:00 P.M.

EVALUATE: (1 week later)
The couple indicated that each felt more positive about himself and his partner.

PINPOINT:
Ambiguity about when intercourse is to occur and who is to initiate it.

RECORD:
Forever.

CONSEQUATE:
Intercourse was to occur four times, with each approaching the other alternately. (Husband was to make the first approach.)

EVALUATE: (1 week later)

Spouses indicated mutual enjoyment, but noted that four times was too often. The alternating approach was maintained, but the number of approaches was not specified.

PINPOINT:

Mr. C. noted that his wife was frequently in a sour mood, which resulted in his becoming very angry.

RECORD:

Four times each week.

CONSEQUATE:

A. Mr. C. was to notice his wife when she was in a good mood. He was to kiss and caress her and tell her that he liked her when she was pleasant.

B. In addition, he was to discuss with her their plans for the week-end.

C. Also, when Mrs. C. exhibited negative behavior, he was to completely ignore her.

EVALUATE: (1 week later)

Mr. C. noted an observable improvement in his wife's mood throughout the next week.

PINPOINT:

Husband complained that wife swore at the children too much.

RECORD:

Constantly, whenever anger occurred.

CONSEQUATE:

A substitute word was to be used where a swear word was previously used, with eating a dessert contingent on the use of the substitute word.

EVALUATE: (1 week later)

Substitute word usage increased and swearing decreased.

PINPOINT:

Mrs. C. complained that her husband did not spend any time with their children.

RECORD:

Zero

CONSEQUATE:

Husband was instructed to spend fifteen minutes of on-task interaction with each of their two children. He was to tell each of them when they would have time with him. During this time period, he was to give his undivided attention to each child, such as reading fairy tales, doing push-ups or cartwheels, or whatever the child chose to do.

EVALUATE: (1 week later)

Husband did spend time with the children which resulted in happy feelings for him, them, and his wife.

PINPOINT:

Mrs. C. complained that her husband cluttered the den each evening by throwing his magazines, books, and newspapers on the floor and on top of the television.

RECORD:

Clutter occurred daily.

CONSEQUATE:

Mr. C. was to clean the den before retiring to bed.

EVALUATE: (1 week later)

Den was cleaned prior to bedtime.

PINPOINT:

It was not clear what responsibilities each partner had daily. As an example, Mrs. C. expected her husband to feed the dog, whereas he expected the same of her.

RECORD:

Incessant

CONSEQUATE:

Each spouse was to draw up a list of what he was responsible for that day and to check off the completion of each of these behaviors before going to bed. Novel reading for Mr. C., dessert for Mrs. C., and sleep for both were made contingent on completing the behaviors on the checklist prior to bedtime.

EVALUATE: (1 week later)

Behaviors on the respective lists occurred. These behaviors resulted in reported mutual happiness.

The couple were seen six months later and indicated they had "slipped a bit." Slipping was defined as their having discontinued consequating their behaviors which resulted in the recurrence of many of the specific behaviors treated in therapy. When each of these behaviors was reinstated, "mutual happiness" recurred.

Happiness occurs in marriage under certain conditions and not under others. When conditions for happiness are identified and maintained, mutual fulfillment results and continues. It is possible that this couple will "slip" again; however, it is their decision and choice to do so. In effect, they may choose between happiness and unhappiness, which may not have been a possibility prior to therapy.

conclusion

The preceding has been concerned with increasing human happiness in marriage. The goal was to illustrate the perspectives and behaviors of the behavior therapist in his attempt to improve conjugal relationships. Marital happiness occurs under certain conditions. The counselor must therefore encourage his clients to consider what behaviors performed by whom, and when, enhance or impede a desirable relationship.

This should be followed by a value commitment of the spouses to increase, decrease, modify, or develop the specified behaviors. Although the client-counselor relationship is a crucial element of therapeutic influence, the counselor must choose carefully his intervention procedures. The techniques outlined in Chapter Three will yield positive marital feelings only if properly applied.

Clients often provide useful guideposts in therapy by selecting from the alternative procedures outlined by the counselor. Records of behavioral changes will direct the continued course of treatment by reflecting needed changes, modifications, etc. Change will occur. The counselor is responsible for directing the course of treatment to achieve the goals (values) of his clients.

Counselors of bewildered spouses know that treatment is difficult. It is easy to pretend that somehow, something will happen to create marital happiness. The behavioral counselor believes that the what, how, when, and who must be objectified and specified. Through these behaviors, happier marriages (and counselors) may result.

appendices

MARRIAGE inventory

PURPOSE OF THIS QUESTIONNAIRE: The purpose of this questionnaire is to obtain a comprehensive picture of you and your marriage. In scientific work, records are necessary, since they permit a more thorough dealing with one's problems. By completing these questions as fully and as accurately as you can, you will facilitate your therapeutic program. You are requested to answer these routine questions on your own time instead of using up your actual consulting time.

It is understandable that you might be concerned about what happens to the information about you, because much or all of this information is highly personal. Case records are strictly confidential. **No outsider is permitted to see your case record without your permission.**

If you do not desire to answer a question, merely write "do not care to answer."

Date _____

1. GENERAL

NAME _____

ADDRESS _____

_____

TELEPHONE NUMBERS: Office _____   Home _____

AGE _____ OCCUPATION _____

BY WHOM WERE YOU REFERRED? _____

_____

WITH WHOM ARE YOU NOW LIVING? (List people) _____

_____

_____

DO YOU LIVE IN A HOUSE, HOTEL, ROOM, APARTMENT,
OR OTHER? _____

MARITAL STATUS: (Circle answer)

SINGLE; ENGAGED; MARRIED; RE-MARRIED; SEPARATED;

DIVORCED; WIDOWED.

2. CLINICAL:

A. **Underline** any of the following words which apply to you:

A "nobody," "life is empty," a "somebody," "life is fun"
Stupid, bright, incompetent, competent, naive, sophisticated
Guilty, at peace with self, horrible thoughts, pleasant
thoughts, hostile, kind, full of hate, full of love
Anxious, panicky, relaxed, cowardly, confident, unassertive,
assertive, aggressive, friendly
Ugly, beautiful, deformed, shapely, attractive, unattractive,
pleasant, repulsive
Depressed, happy, lonely, wanted, needed, unloved, loved,
misunderstood, bored, active, restless
Confused, full of pleasant thoughts about past events
Worthwhile, sympathetic, intelligent, considerate.

139

B.   **Underline** any of the following that apply to you:

Headaches

In love

Content

Nightmares

Elated

Depressed

Unable to relax

Don't like weekends
   and vacations

Can't make friends

Can't keep a job

Fainting spells

No appetite

Insomnia

Alcoholism

Tremors

Dizziness

Stomach trouble

Fatigue

Feel loved

Feel panicky

Suicidal ideas

Over-ambitious

Inferiority feelings

Satisfied

Happy

Take drugs .

Can't make decisions

Unable to have a good time

Concentration difficulties

Others:

3.   **PROBLEM AREAS IN MARRIAGE:**
      Please **underline** each specific problem area which you have
      had or are having in your marriage.
      Include additional information for clarification if necessary.

A.   SEX
      1.   When: A.M., P.M., before supper, etc.
      2.   How:
            a.   Spouse crude in approach
            b.   Too little foreplay
            c.   Other
      3.   Frequency
      4.   Premature ejaculation
      5.   Frigidity
      6.   Infidelity
      7.   Sex information
      8.   Impotence
      9.   Birth control
      10.   Others

B. COMMUNICATION
1. Too little time spent in communicating
2. Nothing to talk about
3. Intellectual gaps
4. Topic or type of conversation (for example, one enjoys gossiping, the other talking about work)
5. How often to communicate when apart
6. Bitching
7. Manner of communication, hasty or impatient
8. Others

C. MONEY
1. Amount: too little, too much
2. Source of money: gambling, borrowing, wife, parents, in-laws, husband, stocks
3. Who spends:
    a. How much
    b. On what
4. Bookkeeping:
    a. Who manages the money
    b. Joint bank account
5. Others

D. IN-LAWS
1. Which ones to visit
2. How much time with parents or in-laws
3. In-laws dislike daughter- or son-in-law, and show it
4. In-laws meddle and try to run children's lives
5. Whether to help in-laws financially
6. Advice from
7. Mate hates partner's parents
8. In-laws do not like each other
9. Others

E. RELIGION
1. Different religions
2. Religion for children
3. One spouse more devout than the other
4. Manner of celebrating holidays
5. Disagreement over religious rituals, (for example, birth control or circumcision)
6. Money to church
7. Unkept vows
8. Others

F. RECREATION
    1. Amount of time for specific recreative activities.
    2. What: disagreement as to type of recreation, (for example, drinking beer, gambling, fishing, shopping, bridge)
    3. Who: solitary or family recreation
    4. When to enjoy recreation (for example, after work or before, on Sunday morning or Saturday)
    5. Where to spend vacation
    6. Competition (for example, "egos" may be hurt if wife is more athletic than husband)
    7. Others

G. FRIENDS
    1. Different friends
    2. Time with
    3. Confidences to friends
    4. Number:
        a. Too few
        b. Too many
    5. Others

H. ALCOHOL
    1. Who drinks
    2. How much alcohol is acceptable
    3. When and where to drink
    4. Amount of money spent on alcohol
    5. What to teach children about alcohol
    6. Certain friends or relatives disapprove of your drinking
    7. Different brands (for example, disagree on the merit of each)
    8. Flirting because of drinking, or general embarrassment or violence
    9. Others

I. CHILDREN
    1. Number
    2. Spacing
    3. Discipline
    4. Time with
    5. Activities child should become involved in
    6. Rivalry for children's love
    7. Sterility or infertility, whether to adopt

8. Retarded or malformed or unwanted child
9. Step-children
10. Sex education
11. Others

4. **What specifically would you like to work on first**? Rank the problems in the order that you would like to deal with them.

5. **What behaviors do you engage in that please your spouse?**

6. **What behaviors does your spouse engage in that please you?**

7. What behaviors do you want to increase or develop in yourself?

8. What behaviors do you want your spouse to increase or develop?

9. Please add any information not tapped by this questionnaire that may aid your therapist in understanding you.

relaxation

Systematic desensitization is one of the more useful techniques of the behavioral clinician. In marriage counseling, it may be used in the treatment of frigidity, impotence, premature ejaculation, fears, and phobias as they affect marital interaction, and an array of other problems where anxiety is present. Just as anxiety is manifested physiologically by an increase in blood pressure and heart rate, relaxation is manifested by the absence of these symptoms. A person who is relaxed, by definition, is not anxious.

To repeat, systematic desensitization involves constructing a hierarchy, training in relaxation, and pairing the state of relaxation with the items on the hierarchy. Relaxation is a prerequisite for desensitization. Although a tension-free body can be effectively induced by hypnosis, the Weitzman procedure (Davison, 1971), or a mixture of carbon dioxide-oxygen, muscle tension release is probably used by most therapists. The induction of relaxation through the release of muscle tension may vary. Wolpe and Lazarus (1966), Turner (1968), Davison (1969), and Madsen (1969) have each developed variants of the other. The writer's procedure that follows (which includes some of the modifications of the above therapists) is derived from Jacobson's (1938) method of relaxation upon which most training sessions of relaxation are based.

PROCEDURE

After the client has been told that relaxation is a most useful therapeutic aid in assisting him with his problem, the counselor dims the light in the counseling room and begins:

At this time, I would like to show you how to relax. What you will be doing is tensing and relaxing each muscle of your body. The procedure is based on the premise that tension and relaxation cannot exist at the same time. If you are relaxed, you cannot be anxious. I want to go through the muscles of the body with you so that when your eyes are closed and I give you verbal cues, you will know exactly what to do. (The therapist models for client what is to follow.)

First, tense your right arm. Tense it just as tightly as you can. Now, relax. I will want you to do that for three times. Then, I will want you to draw up your right arm like Superman, tensing your biceps. We'll do that for three times. Then I want you to straighten your right arm out, tense it, and relax. We will relax your left arm the same way.

With reference to the muscles of your shoulders, I want you to lean forward in the chair, arch your back, and squeeze your shoulder muscles together (three times). For the muscles in the neck, I want you to lift up your neck and tighten the muscles underneath your jawbone. For the muscles of the cheek, I want you to smile very big so that you touch your earlobes with the corners of your mouth. For the lips, I want you to press your lips very tightly together, tensing them together very tightly and relax. For the eyes, I want you to frown and press down on your eyes, and then relax. For the muscles of your forehead, I want you to lift your forehead upward, and then relax.

For the muscles of your chest, stomach, and abdomen, I want you to tense these muscles, then relax. For the muscles of the legs, press the floor with your left foot, tightening the leg muscles, then relax. Then, straighten your leg out, toes pointing outward, then toward your head. You will do the same with your right leg.

Now, I would like for you to get as comfortable in your chair as possible. I would like for you to close your eyes in order to cut off visual stimulation so you will be better able to relax. Just get very comfortable in your chair. With your eyes closed and your arms on the arm rests, just allow your body to become completely supported by the chair. As we begin, I want you to be aware that for the next few minutes, there will be absolutely no demands made on you. The phone isn't going to ring, nobody is coming in, and your children aren't going to bother you. I just want you to allow yourself to become very relaxed in these next few moments.

At this time, I would like for you to take a very deep breath, filling up your lungs with air and allowing the air to flow out all by itself. Take another breath, just as deep as you can and allow the air to flow out all by itself. I would like for you to tense the muscles of the right arm, tense the muscles of your right arm just as tight as you can, tensing, tensing until it almost hurts, and relax. That's the way. Very warm and very comfortable. Let's try it again, Mary. Tense with your right hand, tensing, tensing, and relax. That's the way. You'll be able to feel this warm feeling of relaxation now becoming somewhat present in your right arm. It will feel almost as though it's making its way into the fingertips of your hand. It's a pleasant sensation. Tense the right hand again, tensing, tensing just as tightly as you can, and relax, relax. As we go through this, I want you to be aware of the feeling that you get when you tense and relax each muscle. I do not want you to think yourself into relaxation. I just want you to note the feeling of relaxation that occurs after you tense and relax. Tense once again with the right arm, tensing, tensing until it almost hurts, and relax, relax. Your right arm is feeling very comfortable and warm. Pull up your arm, Mary, at this time and tighten the muscles of your biceps just as tightly as you can. Tense and relax. Tense that same muscle again, tense it until it almost hurts, and relax. Put your arm down now on the arm rest. Feel now that your right arm is relaxed, at ease. . .almost as though it is being supported by the chair.

I would like for you to notice the difference between your right arm and your left arm. Your right arm feels kind of heavy, warm, relaxed, good, and your left arm may be a little cold, tense, and not quite as relaxed as your right arm. Let's bring that feeling of relaxation to your left arm by tensing your left arm at this time, tensing, tensing, tensing until it almost hurts, and relax. That's the way. A very comfortable and warm feeling. You will soon begin to feel this very warm feeling of relaxation which was present in your right arm now making its way into your left arm. Tense the left arm again, tensing, tensing until it almost hurts, and relax, relax. You are almost now beginning to feel this warm feeling of relaxation present in your right arm making its way into your left arm. Tense once again, tensing, tensing, and relax. Now, draw up the muscle in your left hand, tensing your biceps just as tightly as you can. . .tense it until it almost hurts. . .tensing. . .and relax. . .relax. Tense it again, tensing, tensing, and relax. Put your arm down.

I would like for you to straighten both arms out and tense them throughout—tensing, tensing as tightly as you can, tensing, and relax. . .very comfortable and very warm. I'd like for you to take a couple of deep breaths at this time, filling up the lungs, and allowing the air to flow out all by itself. You're feeling very warm now and very comfortable. At this time, I would like for you to lean forward in the chair and arch the muscles of your back, pushing the shoulder muscles together. . .tensing, tensing, and relax, relax. Let s try that again. Tense the muscles of the shoulders, pressing them together just as hard as you can, and relax, relax. One more time. Tense them, tensing, tensing, and relax. Lean back again in the chair. . .you're becoming very comfortable. You can perhaps notice at this time the very warm feeling of relaxation which began in your right hand and has made its way into your left, now comes flowing into your shoulder region. . .warm, comfortable, relaxed, heavy, good.

Thinking now about the muscles of the neck, arch your neck backward and tighten the muscles underneath the neck, tensing them, tensing until it almost hurts, and relax, relax. . .just let the muscles go. Tense the same muscles again underneath the neck, tensing them, tensing just as tightly as you can, tensing, and relax. That's the way. Very comfortable and very warm. Beginning now you feel this very warm feeling flowing into your neck. Now, concentrating on the muscles of the cheeks of the face, I would like for you to try to touch your earlobes with the corners of your mouth, smiling just as big as you can, tensing these muscles, tensing, and relax, relax. Just let the muscles go. Tense the same muscles again, tensing, tensing, tensing, and relax, relax. You are able to feel now this warm feeling of relaxation making its very pronounced way into the head region. Thinking about the muscles of the lips, press them together very tightly, tensing, and relax. That's the way. Very comfortable and very warm. Thinking about the muscles in the eyes, frown just as big as you can; frown just as big as you can, tensing the muscles of the eyes, tensing, and relax, relax. Allow your eyes to become completely relaxed. Tense those muscles again, tensing, and relax, relax.

Thinking about the muscles of your forehead now, lift up your forehead just as high as it will go. Tense those muscles again, upward, upward just as high as you can, tensing, and relax, relax. You feel very good now and are aware of the feeling of relaxation in your arms, shoulders, neck, cheeks, lips, eyes and forehead. . .very relaxed, very comfortable, and very warm. Take another deep breath, just as deep as you can, filling up the lungs with air, and letting the air flow out all by itself. You feel very comfortable, very relaxed, and very warm.

Think about the muscles of the chest, stomach, and abdomen at this time. Tighten them just as tightly as you can, drawing the muscles together, tensing, tensing, and relax, relax. Tighten those muscles again, tensing, tensing, and relax. Tighten those muscles once again. Tense them, tense, and relax, relax. That's the way. You are able now to feel this warm feeling of relaxation which began in your right arm, spread to your left, into the neck and head region, and is now making its way into your chest, stomach, and abdomen. You feel very comfortable and very warm.

Lean forward in the chair, I want you to relax your right leg. Press down on your right leg, tensing, tensing, tensing, and relax, relax. Do that again. . .press downward, tense, and relax, relax. Once again. Press downward, tense, relax. Straighten the leg outward. Pointing the toe outward from you, tense the whole leg, tensing, tensing, tensing, and relax, relax. Press the toe outward again, tensing, tensing, and relax, relax. Point the toe now toward your head just as hard as you can, tensing, and relax, relax. Try that once again, pointing your toes toward your head, tensing, tensing, and relax, relax. Allow your whole right leg now to become very limp.

Thinking about the muscles of your left leg, press downward, tensing, tensing, and relax. Repeat the behavior. Press the left leg downward, tensing, tensing, and relax, relax. Again with the left leg, point the toe outward, tensing, tensing, and relax, relax. Point the toe forward, making the arch just as straight as you can, tensing, tensing, and relax, relax. Point the toe again toward your head, tensing, tensing, and relax, relax. Again point the toe toward the head, and this time tighten the whole left leg, tightening, tensing, tensing, and relax, relax.

Lean back in the chair now. Get completely comfortable and allow the chair to support your complete weight. . .you feel very good. Take a deep breath; fill the lungs with air. Now allow the air to flow out all by iteself. At this time, I would like for you to be aware of tension in any part of your body. As we go through and name each muscle, I want you to make a mental check if tension is present. Think again of the feeling of relaxation that began in your right arm and spread to your left, the shoulder region, neck, cheeks, lips, eyes, and forehead, back into your chest, stomach, and abdomen regions, into your right leg and left leg. At this time, if there is any part of your body that is not relaxed as you would like for it to be, I would like for you to tense and relax those muscles. Tense and relax those muscles. If there is any muscle that is not relaxed as much as you would like for it to be, tense and relax that muscle. Tense and relax.

At this time, I would like for you to stop thinking about being here, stop thinking about being in this office. Instead, think about being on the bow of a sailboat that is being pushed by a gentle breeze over a smooth inland lake. Be able to feel the warm rays of the sun as they touch your skin. It's warm, relaxing, comfortable. You feel very, very comfortable, very, very, relaxed. Think about this scene. Be almost aware of the warm summer rays, feeling very comfortable, very relaxed, very much at ease. I would like for you to stop thinking about being there and think about being here again. Be aware of the feeling of relaxation which you are experiencing.

Stop thinking about being here, and begin to think about lying on the beach. You've been there for several hours now. As you imagine opening your eyes at the beach, you can see a sea gull in the far distance who is making his way very lazily across the blue sky. You can almost hear the waves as they come in and gently touch the shore and move back to sea. Think, at this time, while you're there that you have a portable radio with you and you've just leaned over and turned on the radio to your favorite music. This even enhances your feeling of relaxation while there. I would like for you to stop thinking about being there and think about being here again. Be aware of how relaxed and how comfortable you feel.

Stop thinking about being here and think about yourself lying in a green meadow on a very smooth blanket. You are under the limbs of a towering shade tree on a sunny day. As you look upward, you can see the leaves as they catch the sunlight. Perhaps as you turn your head to one side, you can see tall daisies as they catch the wind and sway gently. A very relaxing scene. The air that you breathe seems very fresh, very outdoors, very enjoyable to you. I would like for you to stop thinking about being there and think about being here again.

I'm going to say the word "calm" at this time, and each time I say the word "calm," I want you to become even more relaxed, even more relaxed, letting all the muscles of your body go. In just a moment, I want you to say the word "calm" also and in situations other than these, you will be able to say the word "calm" which will assist you in returning to this deep state of relaxation which you now feel. I'm going to say the word now and each time that you hear it, I want you to become more aware of your present state of relaxation. Become even more relaxed. Calm. Calm. You're very relaxed, very comfortable. Calm. Calm. Calm. In just a moment, I want you to say the word "calm" and as you say it, be aware of how relaxed, how comfortable you feel. Say the word at this time very slowly. Say it again. Each time you say it, you feel more and more relaxed. Again. You're very comfortable and very relaxed, very, very relaxed. (Desensitization procedure of presenting items on the hierarchy to the subject would begin at this point.)

In just a moment, I'm going to count from ten to zero. When I get to three, open your eyes; when I get to two, prepare to stand up; when I get to zero, stand up.

vibrator

The electric vibrator, often referred to as a massager, has been mentioned as an aid in initiating orgasmic behavior in wives. Since the treatment of frigidity may indicate the advisability of using the vibrator (an unconditioned stimulus), some additional information may be helpful.

There are three types of vibrators (massagers). One type is a small motor that is held on the back of the hand by elastic metal bands. When the massager is turned on, the hand vibrates. This type of massager is used in many barber shops. This massager ranges in price from $15.00 to $60.00 and can be purchased in large department stores such as Sears.

A less expensive massager (about $10.00) is held in the hand and has a vibrating rubber cup. (The cheaper models are as effective as the more expensive models.) Both of these massagers are not to be confused with the penis-shaped battery operated models, sold in drug stores in larger cities for a price of about $7.00. Although sometimes effective, the battery operated vibrator is frequently not capable of providing pervasive intense vibratory sensations necessary for orgasm.

INSTRUCTIONS

In order to insure appropriate use of the electric vibrator, the counselor should share the following concerns with his clients:

1.   **RELAXATION**
       It is crucial for the wife to be relaxed before the vibrator is applied. Wives who are "tense" and "anxious" usually do not achieve a climax with the vibrator and wonder why. Muscle-tension release is often an effective means of inducing relaxation. However, the means of relaxation is not important.

2.   **PLACEMENT**

The vibrator should be placed over the vaginal and clitoral area of the wife. Since the husband does not know what feels best to his wife, she should direct him as to the proper placement of the vibrator to insure pleasurable sensations. If the husband is holding the vibrator too "high" or too "low," the wife should stop his guessing and tell him where it feels best.

3.   **PAIN**

Some women report they experience pain while using the vibrator. This is usually a result of the vibrator being held directly over the clitoris. The extremely intense sensations are interpreted as pain and the vibrator should be moved away from direct contact.

4.   **PATIENCE**

Great differences exist in the way women respond to the vibrator. While some wives will climax within a few seconds, others may require several minutes. However, the vibrator will not produce an orgasm every time. If used 100 times, 85–95 times a climax will be reached, with no result the other 15–5 times. Women who do not experience a climax the first or every time should be patient.

5.   **CAUTION**

Care should be taken never to use the electric vibrator near water. Doing so may produce a deadly shock. In addition, some women have an uncontrollable tendency to urinate at orgasm. For such women, the electric vibrator should not be recommended.

HUSBAND

Caution should be exercised in selecting couples to use the vibrator. One of the important considerations requires a thorough understanding of the attitude of the husband toward the vibrator. A PREREQUISITE for recommending the vibrator is the enthusiastic interest of the husband. Husbands are told that although intercourse may not have resulted in orgasm, the vibrator will. If the husband is hesitant about allowing his wife to achieve an orgasm through using the vibrator or if the counselor judges him to have a low "self concept," the vibrator should not be used. Otherwise, the husband may be threatened by his wife's achieving sexual pleasure by means other than through sexual intercourse with him.

For husbands who are willing to use the vibrator (most are), specific instructions are given as follows: first, to repeat, it is important that the wife be relaxed before using the vibrator over the vaginal region. In addition to muscle tension release, relaxation may result from using the vibrator all over the wife's body. In this way, the vibrator may be used to massage the muscles of the shoulders and back prior to vaginal placement. Second, the husband is instructed to lie on his side with his wife's head in one of his arms while he rests his elbow on his side and his hand over the vaginal area. This instruction is important since many husbands report that they get tired holding the vibrator.

GENERALIZATION TO INTERCOURSE

After enjoying a number of orgasmic experiences in response to the vibrator, most wives want to have an orgasm during intercourse. This can be accomplished by gradually withdrawing the vibrator, replacing it with manual and/or oral stimulation, and finally intercourse. As an example, with the vibrator in place, the wife should tell her husband just before she is about to experience an orgasm. At that time, he should turn off the vibrator and continue to stimulate his wife manually or orally until orgasm occurs. On subsequent occasions, the vibrator should be withdrawn sooner so that manual and/or oral stimulation provides the basis for orgasm. Later, manual and/or oral stimulation is gradually withdrawn and replaced by intercourse in the same way (D'Zurilla, 1971).

The vibrator is a delightful asset to marital sexual fulfillment. Wives who experience no pleasure in sex should be encouraged to consider using the vibrator consistent with the above suggestions. One of the more frequent comments from wives who have begun to use the vibrator is, "It worked. I wish I had known about this before."

references

Arendall, E. M. Dawson Memorial Baptist Church, Birmingham, Alabama. Personal communication, 1971.

Alberti, R. E. and Emmons, M. L. *Your perfect right: A guide to assertive behavior.* San Luis Obispo, California: Impact, 1970.

Anant, S. S. A note on the treatment of alcoholics by verbal aversion techniques. *Canadian Psychologist*, 1967, *8*, 19—22.

Applebaum, S. B. Working wives and mothers. *Public Affairs Pamphlet.* New York: Public Affairs Pamphlets, 1952, No. 188.

Ard, B. N. and Ard, C. C. (Eds.) *Handbook of marriage counseling.* Palo Alto: Science and Behavior Books, Inc., 1969.

Axelson, L. J. Marital adjustment and marital role definitions of husbands of working and non-working wives. *Journal of Marriage and the Family*, 1963, *25,* 190—192.

Bandura, A. *Social learning and personality development.* New York: Holt, Rinehart, and Winston, 1963.

Bandura, A. *Principles of behavior modification.* New York: Holt, Rinehart, and Winston, 1969.

Baron, R. A. and Liebert, R. M. *Human social behavior: A contemporary view of experimental research.* Homewood, Illinois: Dorsey Press, 1971.

Becker, W. C., Madsen, C. H. Jr., Arnold, C. R., and Thomas, D. R. The contingent use of teacher attention and praise in reducing classroom behavior problems. *Journal of Special Education*, 1967, *3*, 287—307.

Blake, B. G. The application of behavior therapy to the treatment of alcoholism. *Behavior Research and Therapy*, 1968, *6*, 389—392.

Blood, R. O., Jr. *Marriage*. New York: Free Press, 1969.

Brady, J. P. Brevital-relaxation of frigidity. *Behavior Research and Therapy*, 1966, *4*, 71—77.

Brown, D. G. Behavior modification in child and school mental health: An annotated bibliography on applications with parents and teachers. 1971. Available from Dr. Brown, National Institute of Mental Health, 50 Seventh Street, N. E., Room 423, Atlanta, Georgia.

Brown, D. G. Female orgasm and sexual inadequacy. In R. Brecher and E. Brecher (Eds.) *An analysis of human sexual response*. New York: New American Library, 1966, Pp. 125—174.

Browning, R. Rabbi ben ezra. In M. H. Abrams (Ed.) *The Norton anthology of English literature*. New York: W. W. Norton and Co., 1962, *2*, 864.

Burgess, E. W. and Cottrell, L. S. *Predicting success or failure in marriage*. Englewood Cliffs, New Jersey. Prentice-Hall, 1939.

Burgess, R. L. and Bushell, D. *Behavioral sociology*. New York: Columbia University Press, 1969.

Cautela, J. R. Covert sensitization. *Psychological Reports*, 1967, *20*, 459—468.

Cautela, J. R. Behavior therapy and self control. In C. M. Franks (Ed.) *Behavior therapy: Appraisal and status*. New York: McGraw-Hill, 1969, Pp. 323—340.

Cautela, J. R. Covert reinforcement. *Behavior Therapy*, 1970, *1*, 33—50.

Cautela, J. R. The treatment of compulsive behavior by covert sensitization. *Psychotherapy*, 1970, in press.

Cooper, A. J. A case of fetishism and impotence treated by behavior therapy. *British Journal of Psychiatry*, 1963, *109*, 649—652.

Croake, J. W. Department of Home and Family Life, Florida State University. Personal communication, 1971.

Davison, G. C. Relaxation tape. State University of New York at Stony Brook, Psychological Services, 1969.

Davison, G. C. Self-control through "imaginal aversive contingency" and "one-downmanship": Enabling the powerless to accommodate unreasonableness. In

J. D. Krumboltz and C. E. Thoresen (Eds.) *Behavioral counseling: Cases and techniques.* New York: Holt, Rinehart, and Winston, 1969, Pp. 319–327.

Davison, G. C. Behavior modification seminar, State University of New York at Stony Brook, 1971.

D'Zurilla, T. J. Group systematic desensitization. Mimeographed paper, 1969.

D'Zurilla, T. J. Reducing heterosexual anxiety. In J. D. Krumboltz and C. E. Thoresen (Eds.) *Behavioral counseling: Cases and techniques.* New York: Holt, Rinehart, and Winston, 1969.

D'Zurilla, T. J. The use of prolonged imagery in the reduction of "neurotic" anxiety. Unpublished manuscript, 1970.

D'Zurilla, T. J. Department of Psychology, State University of New York at Stony Brook. Personal communication, 1971.

Eastman, W. F. Department of Psychiatry, University of North Carolina, Chapel Hill, North Carolina. Personal communication, 1971.

Ellis, A. *Reason and emotion in psychotherapy.* New York: Lyle Stuart, 1962.

Family life and sex education. A course outline for Anaheim Union High School, Anaheim, California, 1966.

Farber, B. Family organization and crisis. *Research in Child Development,* 1960.

Feldman, M. P. Aversion therapy for sexual deviations: A critical review. *Psychological Bulletin,* 1966, 65–80.

Fensterheim, H. *Case report: Assertive methods and marital problems.* Unpublished manuscript, 1970.

Festinger, L. A. *A theory of cognitive dissonance.* Stanford: Stanford University Press, 1962.

Frankl, V. Paradoxical intention, a logotherapeutic technique. *American Journal of Psychotherapy,* 1960, *14,* 520.

Franks, C. M. (Ed.) *Behavior therapy: Appraisal and status.* New York: McGraw-Hill, 1969.

Friedman, D. The treatment of impotence by Brevital relaxation therapy. *Behavior Research and Therapy,* 1968, *6,* 257–261.

Goldberg, B. Department of Psychology, State University of New York at Stony Brook. Personal communication, 1971.

Goldfried, M. R. and Pomeranz, D. M. Role of assessment in behavior modification. *Psychological Reports,* 1968, *23,* 75–87.

Goldstein, M. K. and Francis, B. Behavior modification of husbands by wives. Paper, National Council on Family Relations, Washington, D. C., 1969.

Greene, J. T. Department of Sociology, Florida State University. Personal communication, 1970.

Guest, E. A. Sermons we see. *The light of fate*. Chicago: Reilly and Lee, 1926.

Hagerty, E. Department of Family Relations, University of British Columbia. Personal communication, 1971.

Hastings, D. W. Can specific training procedures overcome sexual inadequacy? In R. Brecher and E. Brecher (Eds.) *An analysis of human sexual response*. New York: The New American Library, 1966, 221–235.

Homme, L. E. Perspectives in psychology: XXIV control of coverants, the operants of the mind. *The Psychological Record*, 1965, *15*, 501–511.

Homme, L. E., Homme, A., C'de Baca, P., and Cottingham, L. What behavioral engineering is. *The Psychological Record*, 1968, *18*, 425–434.

"J" *The sensuous woman*. New York: Lyle Stuart, 1969.

Jacobson, E. *Progressive relaxation*. Chicago: University of Chicago Press, 1938.

Johnson, E. F., Jr., Department of Sociology, Florida State University. Personal communication, 1971.

King, K., McIntyre, J., and Axelson, L. J. Adolescent views of maternal employment as a threat to the marital relationship. *Journal of Marriage and the Family*, 1968, *30*, 633–673.

Kinsey, A. C., Pomeroy, W. B., and Martin, C. F. *Sexual behavior in the human male*. Philadelphia: Saunders, 1948.

Kinsey, A. C., Pomeroy, W. B., and Martin, C. F. *Sexual behavior in the human female*. Philadelphia: Saunders, 1953.

Kirkendall, L. A. Helping children understand sex. *Better Living Booklet*, New York: Science Research Associates, 1952.

Klemer, R. H. (Ed.) *Counseling in marital and sexual problems*. Baltimore: Williams and Williams, 1965.

Klemer, R. H. *Marriage and family relationships*. New York: Harper and Row, 1970.

Knox, D. Attitudes toward love of high school seniors. *Adolescence*, 1970, *5*, 89–100.

Knox, D. Conceptions of love of married college students. *College Student Survey*, 1970, *4*, 28–30.

Knox, D. Conceptions of love at three developmental levels. *The Family Coordinator*, 1970, *19*, 151—157.

Knox, D. Intercourse—how often? *Sexology*, July, 1970.

Knox, D. Behavior therapy and marriage problems. Paper, National Council on Family Relations, Chicago, 1970.

Knox, D. *A discussion guide to accompany the love attitude inventory*. Saluda, North Carolina: Family Life Publications, 1971.

Knox, D. *Keeping happiness in your marriage*. Champaign, Illinois: Research Press Co., 1972.

Knox, D. and Patrick, J. A. You are what you do: A new approach in preparation for marriage. *The Family Coordinator*, 1971, *20*, 109—114.

Knox, D. and Sporakowski, M. J. Attitudes of college students toward love. *Journal of Marriage and the Family*, 1968, *30*, 638—642.

Kraft, T. and Al-Issa, I. Alcoholism treated by desensitization: A case report. *Behavior Research and Therapy*, 1967, *5*, 69—70.

Kraft, T. and Al-Issa, I. The use of methohexitone sodium in the systematic desensitization of premature ejaculation. *British Journal of Psychiatry*, 1968, *114*, 351—352.

Krasner, L. The therapist as a reinforcement machine. In H. H. Strupp and L. Luborsky (Eds.) *Research in Psychotherapy*, 1962, American Psychological Association.

Krasner, L. The behavioral scientist and social responsibility: No place to hide. *Journal of Social Issues*, 1965, *21*, 9—30.

Krasner, L. Behavior therapy. *Annual Review of Psychology*, 1971, *22*, 483—531.

Lazarus, A. A. The treatment of chronic frigidity by systematic desensitization. *Journal of Nervous and Mental Disease*, 1963, *136*, 272—278.

Lazarus, A. A. The treatment of a sexually inadequate man. In L. P. Ullmann and L. Krasner (Eds.) *Case studies in behavior modification*. New York: Holt, Rinehart, and Winston, 1965. Pp. 243—245.

Lazarus, A. A. Behavioral rehearsal vs. non-directive therapy vs. advice in effecting behavior change. *Behavior Research and Therapy*, 1966, *4*, 209—212.

Lazarus, A. A. Behavior therapy and marriage counseling. *Journal of the American Society of Psychosomatic Dentistry and Medicine*, 1968, *15*, 49—56.

Lazarus, A. A. Rehearsal desensitization. *Psychotherapy*, 1968.

Lazarus, A. A. Department of Psychology, Yale University. Personal communication, 1970.

Lazarus, A. A. *Behavior therapy and beyond*. New York: McGraw-Hill, 1971.

Lazarus, A. A. and Serber, M. Is systematic desensitization being misapplied? *Psychological Reports*, 1968, *23,* 215–218.

Lederer, W. J. and Jackson, D. D. *The mirages of marriage*. New York: W. W. Norton, 1968.

Leslie, G. R. The field of marriage counseling. In H. T. Christensen (Ed.) *Handbook of marriage and the family*. Chicago: Rand McNally, 1964.

Liberman, R. Behavioral approaches to family and couple therapy. *American Journal of Orthopsychiatry*, 1970, *40,* 106–118.

Liebert, R. M. and Fernandez, Luis E. Effects of vicarious consequences on imitative performance. *Child Development*, 1970, *41,* 847–852.

Lindsley, O. R. Teaching teachers to teach. Paper, American Psychological Association Convention, New York, 1966.

Locke, H. J. and Mackprange, M. Marital adjustment and the employed wife. *American Journal of Sociology*, 1949, *54,* 536–545.

Lovibond, S. H. and Caddy, G. Discriminated aversive control in the moderation of alcoholic's drinking behavior. *Behavior Therapy*, 1970, *1,* 437–444.

Lubetkin, B. S., Rivers, P. C., and Rosenberg, C. M. Difficulties of disulfiram therapy with alcoholics. *Quarterly Journal of Studies on Alcohol*, 1971, *32,* 168–171.

Mace, D. and Mace, V. *Marriage: East and west*. New York: Doubleday, 1960.

Madsen, C. H. Jr. Department of Psychology, Florida State University. Personal communications, 1968, 1969, 1970.

Madsen, C. H. Jr., Becker, W. C., and Thomas, D. R. Rules, praise, and ignoring: Elements of elementary classroom control. *Journal of Applied Behavior Analysis*, 1968, *1,* 139–150.

Madsen, C. H., Jr. and Madsen, C. K. *Teaching/discipline: Behavioral principles toward a positive approach*. Boston: Allyn and Bacon, 1970.

Madsen, C. H., Jr. and Madsen, C. K. *Parents/children/discipline—a positive way*. Boston: Allyn and Bacon, 1971.

Masters, W. H. and Johnson, V. E. *Human sexual response*. Boston: Little, Brown, 1966.

Masters, W. H. and Johnson, V. E. *Human sexual inadequacy*. Boston: Little, Brown, 1970.

McCary, J. L. *Human sexuality*. New York: Van Nostrand, 1967.

McFall, R. M. and Marston, A. R. An experimental investigation of behavior rehearsal in assertive training. *Journal of Abnormal Psychology*, 1970, *76*, 295–303.

McGee, J. P., Milgram, N. and Reidel, W. Prediction of performance by retardates and non-retarded. *American Journal of Mental Deficiency*, March, 1970.

Mead, M. *Sex and temperament in three primitive societies*. New York: New American Library, 1938.

Mead, M. *Male and female*. New York: New American Library, 1949.

Middleton, J. College of Arts and Sciences, State University of New York at Plattsburg. Personal communication, 1968.

Mills, K. C., Sobell, M. B., and Schaefer, H. H. Training social drinking as an alternative to abstinence for alcoholics. *Behavior Therapy*, 1971, *2*, 18–27.

Nash, E. M., Jessner, L., and Abse, D. W. (Eds.) *Marriage counseling in medical practice*. Chapel Hill: The University of North Carolina Press, 1964.

Nawas, M. M., Fishman, S. T., and Pucel, J. C. A standardized desensitization program applicable to group and individual treatments. *Behavior Research and Therapy*, 1970, *8*, 49–56.

Nawas, M. M., Mealiea, W. C., and Fishman, S. T. Systematic desensitization as counter-conditioning: A retest with adequate controls. *Behavior Therapy*, 1971, in press.

Olson, D. H. Marital and family therapy: Integrative review and critique. *Journal of Marriage and the Family*, 1970, *32*, 501–538.

Patterson, G. R. and Gullion, M. E. *Living with children*. Champaign, Illinois: Research Press Co., 1968.

Paul, G. L. Paper, American Psychological Association Convention, New York, 1966.

Peterson, J. A. (Ed.) *Marriage and family counseling: Perspective and prospect*. New York: Association Press, 1968.

Premack, D. Toward empirical behavioral laws: I. Positive reinforcement. *Psychological Review*, 1959, *66*, 219–333.

Premack, D. Reinforcement theory. In D. Levine (Ed.) Nebraska symposium on motivation. Lincoln: University of Nebraska Press, 1965, 123–180.

Rachman, S. and Teasdale, J. D. Aversion therapy: An appraisal. In C. M. Franks (Ed.) *Behavior therapy: Appraisal and status*. New York: McGraw-Hill, 1969.

Rappaport, A. F. and Harrell, J. A. *A behavioral-exchange model for marital counseling*. Family Consultation Center of the College of Human Development, Pennsylvania State University, 1971.

Salter, A. *Conditioned reflex therapy*. New York: Capricorn Books, 1961.

Satir, V. *Conjoint family therapy*. Palo Alto, California: Science and Behavior Books, 1967.

Semans, J. H. Premature ejaculation: A new approach. *Southern Medical Journal*, 1956, *49,* 353—357.

Silverman, H. L. (Ed.) *Marital counseling*. Springfield, Illinois: Charles C. Thomas, 1967.

Simkins, L. The reliability of self-recorded behaviors. *Behavior Therapy*, 1971, *2,* 83—87.

Stampfl, T. G. and Levis, D. J. Essentials of implosive therapy: a learning-theory-based psychodynamic behavioral therapy. *Journal of Abnormal Psychology*, 1967, *72,* 496—503.

Stephens, W. N. *The family in cross-cultural perspective*. New York: Holt, Rinehart, and Winston, 1957.

Stuart, R. B. Operant-interpersonal treatment for marital discord. *Journal of Consulting and Clinical Psychology*, 1969, *33,* 675—682.

Stuart, R. B. Regional workshop on behavior modification applied to marriage counseling, National Institute of Mental Health, Huntsville, Alabama, June, 1971.

Turner, A. J. Huntsville-Madison County Mental Health Center, Huntsville, Alabama. Personal communication, 1971.

Thomas, E. J., Carter, R. D., and Gambrill, E. D. Some possibilities on behavior modification with marital problems using "SAM" (signal system for the assessment and modification of behavior). Paper, Association for Advancement of Behavior Therapy, Washington, D. C., 1969.

Ullmann, L. P. and Krasner, L. *Case studies in behavior modification*. New York: Holt, Rinehart, and Winston, 1965.

Ullmann, L. P. and Krasner, L. *A psychological approach to abnormal behavior*. Englewood Cliffs, New Jersey: Prentice-Hall, 1969.

Weiss, R. Regional workshop on behavior modification applied to marriage counseling, National Institute of Mental Health, Huntsville, Alabama, June, 1971.

Wickramasekera, I. Desensitization, re-sensitization, and desensitization again: A preliminary study. *Journal of Behavior Therapy and Experimental Psychiatry*, 1970, *1,* 257—262.

Wilson, G. T. and Davison, G. C. Aversion techniques in behavior therapy: Some theoretical and metatheoretical considerations. *Journal of Consulting and Clinical Psychology*, 1969, *33,* 327—329.

Wolpe, J. *The practice of behavior therapy*. New York: Pergamon Press, 1969.

Wolpe, J. and Lazarus, A. A. *Behavior therapy techniques: A guide to the treatment of neuroses*. New York: Pergamon Press, 1966.

Wright, J., Jr. Department of Sociology, Mississippi State University, State College, Mississippi. Personal communication, 1971.

index

C

D

E

F

R

S

T

Y